# Kerala:
# Another Possible World

# Kerala:
# Another Possible World

T.M. Thomas Isaac

LeftWord

First published in April 2022
Reprinted November 2022

LeftWord Books
2254/2A, Shadi Khampur
New Ranjit Nagar
New Delhi 110008
INDIA

LeftWord Books and Vaam Prakashan are imprints of
Naya Rasta Publishers Pvt. Ltd.

leftword.com

ISBN 978-93-92018-32-9 (paperback)
978-93-92018-37-4 (e-book)



Printed and bound by Chaman Enterprises, New Delhi.

Visit website

**Contents**

## Acknowledgements

'There is no alternative (TINA)' has been the slogan of the neoliberals ever since the collapse of the Soviet Union. The counter-slogan has been, 'Another world is possible'. Here is the story of the ongoing struggles to build 'another world' in Kerala, India. Hence the title of this book, *Kerala: Another Possible World.*

It was comrade Vijay Prashad who persuaded me to write this book as there was a lot of interest nationally and internationally to understand the socio-economic developments in Kerala. His condition was that the book should be small and non-technical. He has been pushing me to write for the last one year and this is the outcome. Many developments have taken place after the first draft of the book was written six months ago. I thought it would be better to reserve them for the next edition.

I thank Prof. A.V. Jose, Prof. K.J. Joseph and Gopakumar Mukundan for their comments on the draft manuscript. Dr Kiran K. Kakarlapudi helped to tabulate the data. K.G. Biju helped to analyse the electoral data. I have also benefited from discussions with scholars in the Gulati Institute of Finance and Taxation. S. Rananath has shouldered the responsibility for typing.

I thank Devi Vijay for her excellent comments and edits; Akash Sheshadri for his striking cover design; and Sudhanva Deshpande, Winnie Chauhan, and the entire LeftWord Books team for the care and attention given to this book.

T.M. Thomas Isaac
Distinguished Honorary Fellow
Gulati Institute of Finance and Taxation

Chapter 1

# The Kerala Experience in Engaging with the Neoliberal Federal System

Two recent events have brought public attention to the politics and economics of the Indian state of Kerala. With a population of 35 million, Kerala is on the southwest fringe of the Indian subcontinent. The first event was the state's success in containing the spread of the Covid-19 pandemic and the fatality due to the disease during its first wave. Kerala's health minister was celebrated as a Corona Slayer and a Rockstar. The second event was the electoral victory of the Left Democratic Front (LDF) in the 2021 election to the state legislative assembly, giving a second term to the government led by Chief Minister Pinarayi Vijayan. The electoral victory bucked the trend: within Kerala, it was for the first time during the last four decades that a government, Left or right, was re-elected after completing a term. After a series of setbacks in its strongholds at the national level, the Left savoured an electoral victory.

It was not for the first time that the state was attracting international attention. The newly formed united Kerala, the homeland of Malayalam-speaking people, startled the world in 1957 by electing Communists to government, one of the first such instances in history. Given the cold war global environment, the US anticipated a possible domino effect and supported a violent agitation by the opposition, which finally succeeded in ousting the government through the intervention of the central government in New Delhi. Kerala was, in their eyes, the problem state of India.

The state once again came into the limelight with the publication of the study *Poverty, Unemployment and Development*

*Policy* by the Centre for Development Studies (CDS) in 1975. This text highlighted a rather unique development experience. Though economically backward, Kerala provided a much better quality of life for its ordinary people: all children go to school, and people are better educated; people are healthier and live longer; they are better sheltered and fed; and most people are provided with social security. It was a case of successful redistribution; its varied aspects were widely discussed in academic circles. It was the Left who unionised workers for better wages and mobilised peasants for land reforms, the two major redistributive measures. The social movements for education, health care, and basic needs had a much longer history, but the Left played an important role in taking forward these demands. Therefore, the legacy of redistributive gains was an essential part of the Left narrative and a cause of popular support.

Unlike the discussions about development — such as those provoked by the CDS report — which were primarily confined to the academic domain, the recent successes in containing COVID-19 and re-election of the state government have attracted widespread attention. In the context of a national epidemic of communalism, the question is asked: what makes the state of Kerala more resistant not only to the pandemic but also to the social virus of communalism and neoliberalism? What enabled Kerala to buck the trend?

## THE CHALLENGE OF NEOLIBERAL GLOBALISATION

The fall of the Soviet Union and the emergence of neoliberal globalisation have been significant setbacks for radical movements worldwide. The trade union movement has steadily weakened because of the internationalization of production and restructuring of the workforce towards greater informalization. The nation-states have little control over the cross-border movement of capital, goods, and services. Possibilities of autonomous development paths are increasingly foreclosed. In Latin American countries, people fed up with the continuous decline in income and living standards due to the World Bank–International Monetary Fund structural adjustment programs, turned to Left alternatives during the 1990s in the 'Pink Tide' revolutionary wave. Yet these movements could not be sustained. The measures adopted in many of these countries included land reforms, promotion of education and public health, and democratic decentralisation, similar to the Left initiatives in Kerala. And Kerala, unlike these countries, is only a state within the federal Indian union and therefore even more constrained in pursuing an autonomous development path. How did Kerala engage with the neoliberal regime in India?

Following independence in 1947, India adopted a capitalist development path grounded in state planning, where the productive forces were led by the public sector and were cushioned by import substitution. To overcome India's domestic market constraints, the governments of the 1980s attempted to shift towards an export-oriented growth strategy supported by foreign loans and imports. By 1991, the country was in a major foreign exchange crisis and adopted the World Bank–International Monetary Fund programme of import liberalisation, devaluations, fiscal consolidation, and structural adjustment. The structural adjustment in many sectors — as in financial sector liberalisation, labour law reforms, and public sector privatisation — have been slow due to determined resistance from the trade union movement. Yet, the political environment has decisively shifted in favour of neoliberalism, with both major national parties — the BJP and the Congress — swearing by it. The regional parties which are in power in many of the states have shifted to neoliberal programmes. The Left is the only political formation that has adopted a consistent adversarial position to the neoliberal regime. But during the past two decades, the Left has lost power in Bengal and Tripura and has been weakened in most other states.

The impact of the neoliberal regime in India has varied from region to region. The interstate inequalities have tended to widen during this period. Kerala has perhaps been affected worst by the new policies. Its agricultural sector mainly consisted of commercial crops like rubber, coconut, tea, coffee, and spices. These thrived under the earlier protection regime but struggled when opened to direct competition from imports from Sri Lanka and other South Asian countries. In the free trade agreement with ASEAN, Kerala's agricultural interests were sacrificed for the advantage of market access for India's service industry. Not only was no compensatory support given to Kerala's agriculturalists, but even the existing Commodity Board regulations are being dismantled. As a result, we see later in the book that Kerala's agricultural sector has been devastated.

The fall in prices of Kerala's main export products was paralleled by a rise in the prices of its main imports. Rice supplied through the public distribution system at subsidised prices, and steel, cement, petroleum products, and other essential, intermediate goods whose prices were regulated were the major items of import into Kerala apart from consumer products. Price controls were removed as part of the deregulation, and universal statutory rationing ended. The result was that the terms of trade for the state, which in the past were in favour of Kerala, sharply deteriorated with serious adverse growth and welfare implications.

The Indian government's 2003 Fiscal Responsibility and Budget Management (FRMB) Act imposed restrictions on public borrowing by the state government to 3 per cent of the Gross State Domestic Product (GSDP) and the revenue expenditure to the revenue earning capacity. In other words, borrowed funds could not be used for revenue expenditure on education, healthcare, and other social sectors. The revenue deficit had to be reduced to zero. The introduction of a national Goods and Service Tax (GST) on 1 July 2017 subsumed most of the indirect taxes of the states and Union Government, severely restricting the fiscal autonomy for additional resource mobilisation. To further add to the state government's fiscal problems, the central transfers to Kerala drastically declined because of the norms adopted by Union Finance Commissions. The two important criteria for devolution to states were — population share and social indicators of backwardness. With a declining population and improving social indicators, Kerala was disadvantaged (Isaac et al., 2019).

National planning was abolished, and market forces came into full play. A state like Kerala in the geographical corner of India, without adequate infrastructure, strong trade unions, and a lacklustre record in industrialization, was at a disadvantage in attracting investment.

According to the Constitution, India though a Union of States, is a quasi-federal system. The Union Government continuously made inroads into the states' legislative, financial, and administrative domains. This centralisation tendency peaked during the neoliberal period. More and more subjects were transferred from the States list to the concurrent or Union Lists. International treaties in the subject domains of the states were signed without consultation with the respective states. At the extreme, the state of Jammu and Kashmir was divided into three union territories. Even statehood was at the mercy of the Union.

Under this extremely restrictive federal framework, Kerala has been evolving its Left alternative. The present book is an attempt to survey Kerala's success in challenging the neoliberal federal system. One cannot wish away the concrete reality but must work within the system while mobilising people in favour of alternatives and raising their confidence with the successes, however limited they might be. Kerala's own past record in this regard is positive. Even during the colonial period, the social movements, unlike the rest of India, did succeed in achieving education and health improvement. If it can be achieved within a colonial framework, we can be confident to identify some circle of autonomy for the popular forces to intervene and put forth their alternatives at any level of globalisation. It is these contemporary processes that we shall mainly survey.

## RESPONSE OF KERALA — AN OUTLINE

The Left Alternative in Kerala has its deep roots in the history of the national movement, social reforms, and class organisations. In chapter 2, we draw attention to the successful application of the dialectical approach to problems of Kerala society that enabled the Left to rise to the leadership of the national movement in the region, attract the radical and dynamic elements of the social reform movement, and build up class and mass organisations. The Left's role in the movement for a united Kerala and its cultural interventions also enabled the Left forces to become a hegemonic force and form the government in 1957.

The 1957 Communist ministry was a galaxy of the best of the Malayali leadership, and it made deep imprints on almost all aspects of Kerala's society and economy. However, the alternative crafted by the Left cannot be explained merely by reference to historical traditions. The influence of the Left has witnessed drastic erosion even in regions that can take pride in equally strong traditions. A significant portion of chapter 3 on the growth of the Left in the post-independence period is about the stagnation of the electoral strength of the movement in Kerala from the 1980s. The consecutive victory of the Left in 2021 may be a signal of the success of the Left in overcoming some of the impediments to expanding its influence.

The social mobilisation of the Left is based on partial demands related to civic rights and livelihood. They are more concerned with the distribution of wealth and income than their production. In Chapter 4, we examine the contribution of the Leftist redistribution strategy in the making of what has come to be known euphemistically as the 'Kerala Model' — a better life for ordinary people even at a low level of production. The model already faced serious doubts regarding its sustainability in the absence of robust economic growth when the neoliberal regime turned everything topsy turvy.

Therefore, in Chapter 5, we share an overview of the evolution of the economic base. After four decades of stagnation from the late 1980s, the economic growth accelerated so that the Kerala's economy was transformed from a low per capita income-low consumption-low saving economy into a high per capita income-high consumption-high saving economy. The prime mover in this transformation was international migration, facilitated by the much better human resources of the state and resultant remittance inflow. However, from the late 1990s, the state has faced agriculture collapse and a growing fiscal crisis. A new strategy was required to promote agriculture and the development of tiny-small scale industries and the improvement of the quality of services.

Democratic decentralisation was the answer through the People's Planning Campaign (PPC) (1996–2001). As we shall discuss in Chapter 6, it was distinct from the decentralisation programs sponsored by the World Bank as part of their structural reforms in Third World countries. The PPC drew inspiration from the national movement, placed local planning at the centre, devolved proportionate finance and functionaries, and replaced privatisation with participation. And unlike most of the World Bank-sponsored programs, decentralisation in Kerala has positively impacted asset creation, quality of services, poverty reduction, and to a lesser extent on the production sectors.

In Chapter 7, we turn our attention to how the LDF government (2016–2021) addressed the COVID-19 challenge. Kerala has one of the lowest spreads of COVID-19, as revealed by the serosurveillance survey and the lowest fatality rate in the country. The comprehensive intervention program included expanding COVID-19 health care at different levels to keep ahead of the pandemic curve; extensive relief program which included cash transfer, monthly food kit, and consumption loans. The state laid down a detailed protocol for regulating social behaviour, which was by and large voluntarily complied with by the majority of people. In the context of repeated crises of floods and the pandemic, social programmes targeting ordinary people scaled new heights. The crises also underlined a new source of strength for Kerala society: the empowered local governments.

The fiscal crisis of the state government because of COVID-19 did not adversely impact the infrastructure investment because of the innovation of a financial institution to mobilise resources outside the budget and implement projects through special purpose vehicles. Chapter 8 discusses the Kerala Infrastructure Investment Fund Board (KIIFB) and the successful launch of a Rs 60,000 crores infrastructure programme that would overcome the historical infrastructural deficit of the state. The completion of nearly 20 per cent of the projects itself created a euphoria in the state.

The LDF government that has been re-elected in 2021 can today confidently put forward a program for transforming the economic base of Kerala. The 2021–22 budget has unveiled a program for transformation to a knowledge economy. It would involve increasing the knowledge intensity of existing agriculture and other enterprises, attracting investors into knowledge-skill-service-based industries, promoting start-ups, and taking advantage of the trend towards working from home in the global economy to provide jobs to educated unemployed. It would involve overhauling the higher education in the state. The role that school education played in the first phase of Kerala development will now be played by higher education in the current stage of development.

Thus, we conclude the book in Chapter 10. We shall briefly touch on the social alliance that the above program implies. The neoliberal shift has accelerated the growth of a new middle class whose aspirations are quite different from the traditional middle class. At one level, they have been a source for a resurgence of caste and communal trends and the strengthening of right-wing ideologies in the state. At the same time, their numbers are substantial, and many below aspire to join them. The big question is if the new programme of welfare, infrastructure and knowledge economy will enable a broad alliance of the traditional class base of the Left and the new middle class. What would be the implications of the success of this strategy for the future of the Left in Kerala? How will it influence the strengthening of the Left movement in India? What possible lessons can be learnt from Kerala to build another possible world in other parts of the globe?

Chapter 2

# The Making of Communist Hegemony in Kerala

The Communist Party emerged in Kerala relatively late, nearly two decades after the appearance of the first communist groups on the Indian political horizon. In October 1939, a secret conference of the Congress Socialist Party leaders of Malabar resolved to transform their organisation into a unit of the Communist Party of India. On 26 January 1940, on the tenth anniversary of the declaration of independence as the Congress goal, the new party announced its existence through a massive wall writing campaign.[1]

The late formation of the CPI in Kerala might appear somewhat surprising given that it was in Malayalam that one of the earliest biographies of Marx in any Indian language came to be published. The industrial backwardness of the region and consequent weakness of the working-class movement was an important reason for its late formation. The national movement was weak until the third decade of the twentieth century.

In Kerala, political life remained in deep slumber after the anti-British feudal and peasant revolts during the nineteenth century. The Non-Cooperation and Khilafat movements in Malabar drew large sections of the peasantry, especially the Mappila tenants, into the path of agitation. Unfortunately, the militant agitation of the Muslim peasantry in South Malabar developed communal overtones, which enabled the British to repress it most viciously. The Muslim community withdrew into a social cocoon and the upper caste leadership of the national movement, fearful of a

[1] The discussion in this chapter is based mainly on these sources: Namboodiripad (1984, 1986, 1987, 1994); Communist Party of India (Marxist) (2018, 2019, 2020); and Isaac (1986)

repetition of the so-called Mappila Revolt of 1921, slipped into a period of inactivity.

Even before the advent of the national movement, powerful social reform movements swept through all the castes and communities, challenging the outmoded customs and practices. The movements of oppressed castes were also directed against caste discrimination and exploitation. Yet another stream of social mobilisation was the emergence and spread of class-based movements of workers and peasants. The Communist movement in Kerala was drawn from the best elements of these three streams, each of which is briefly discussed in the subsequent sections.

## NATIONAL MOVEMENT AND CONGRESS SOCIALIST PARTY (CSP) IN MALABAR

The Civil Disobedience Movement of 1930 galvanised Malabar into action and saw the emergence of a new generation of young leaders such as K. Kelappan, E.M.S. Namboodiripad, A.K. Gopalan, and P. Krishnapillai. The personal heroism and enthusiasm of the young Gandhian satyagrahis breaking the salt law or picketing foreign cloth shops and liquor shops drew widespread attention. However, to their great disappointment, Gandhiji withdrew the national struggle because it had transgressed the boundaries of his passive resistance tactics. The movement was diverted into constructive work and Harijan Welfare programs without direct linkage with the anti-British struggle.

The search for an alternative by the disillusioned nationalists attracted them to the CSP platform that was emerging at the national level as a Left pressure group within Congress. The CSP and CPI collaborated at the national level, and many communist leaders were active in CSP. The CSP activists in Malabar tended to gravitate towards the communist group. The most crucial factor that influenced this shift was the deep respect they had developed towards the achievements of the Soviet Union. The Kerala region with relatively higher levels of commercialised agriculture was in the throes of depression, like the rest of the capitalist world. The Soviet Union presented a sharp contrast. The secret CPI unit of five leading cadres of the CSP in Malabar, formed in 1937, also played an important role in rapidly disseminating Marxist-Leninist ideology within the movement.

The need for a new type of organisation with ideological clarity was a deeply felt need of the CSP activists. It was clear that the platform of the CSP working within the organisational discipline and programmatic understanding of the Kerala Pradesh Congress Committee (KPCC) was becoming a hindrance to the further growth of the class organisations in Malabar. For example, the peasant movement in northern Malabar that had developed into a no-rent campaign had to be diverted into a campaign for amending the Tenancy Act. The reason was that it was not possible to raise the slogan of the abolition of landlordism from the platform of Congress.

Nevertheless, the CSP succeeded greatly in transforming the Congress into a genuine anti-imperialist united front. It was achieved through a determined struggle against the Gandhian right within Congress, who tried by every manner to prevent the ascendancy of the CSP and the independent growth of class and mass organisations. They finally ousted the CSP from the leadership of the Kerala Pradesh Congress Committee (KPCC) in 1934.

However, with consistent work at the grass-root level and the tactical alliance with the nationalist Muslim faction within the Congress, the CSP was again able to capture the leadership of the KPCC in 1938. With the outbreak of the War and the CPI tactics of unconditional resistance to war efforts, the struggle between the Gandhians and the socialists reached a new high pitch. It was accompanied by the ascendancy of peasant and workers' agitations as well as widespread police repression in Malabar. Mass mobilisation, conducted despite the disapproval of the right-inclined leadership for Anti-Repression Day on 15 September 1939, led to violent confrontations in many centres with the police. The incidents provided the rightists with an opportunity to carry out a purge to cleanse the Congress organisation of the communists: the Malabar District Committee of the KPCC was disbanded, the Leftist KPCC was superseded, and the rightists placed firmly in the saddle. The organisational break of CPI and Congress in Malabar was complete. In a sense, they were fortunate in escaping the phase of extreme sectarianism that characterised the tactics of the CPI at the end of the 'twenties. By the time the break with the Congress occurred, the Communists were recognised as leaders of the national movement.

## THE SOCIAL REFORM MOVEMENTS AND THE COMMUNIST PARTY

From Congress Gandhians to Congress Socialists and thence to Communists: such was the path traversed by the radical nationalists of Malabar in the 1920s and 1930s. The transition in the princely states of Travancore and Cochin was primarily from social reform activism to radical nationalism and thence to Communism.

The background to the social reform movements was the disruption of the traditional agrarian economy by the rapid expansion of commercial agriculture, the rise of agro-processing industries, and trade. Consequently, new social strata of traders, manufacturers, and the middle class emerged, which undermined the caste-class identity of the traditional agrarian society. In Table 2.1 (overleaf) we sum up the caste and agrarian hierarchy in traditional Kerala society. Each community's position in the agrarian hierarchical order roughly corresponded to their position in the social or caste hierarchy.

The new classes emerged not from the upper castes but from the middle castes or non-Hindu communities, disrupting the

**Table 2.1 Caste and Agrarian Hierarchy in Traditional Kerala Society**

| | | |
|---|---|---|
| Priests, Rulers, Administrative Officials | The Landlords | Brahmins, Rajas, Aristocratic Nairs |
| Militia, In-charge of Law and Order, Petty Officials | Superior Tenants | Nairs and Nambiars |
| Petty Producers, Traders, Artisans, Dry Land Labour | Tenants at will | Non-aristocratic Nairs, Ezhavas, Christians and Muslims |
| Wet-land Labour | Agriculture Labour | Ezhavas, Pulayas, Cherumas |

Source: Isaac and Tharakan, 1986.

traditional caste–class identity. The conventional caste hierarchy and domination by the upper castes became a hindrance to the upward mobility of the new classes. The outmoded customs and rituals in every caste and community also became anachronisms in the age of the acquisitive economy that was growing. It was an age pregnant with social contradictions.

Anecdotes of these contradictions are abundant. The first coir factory setup in the Alleppey beach by an Irish American (James Darragh) could not get sufficient workers to work, where traditional pollution norms could not be maintained. One of the wealthiest Travancoreans hailing from a backward caste (Alummoottil Channar) could not drive through the temple road in his native Mavelikkara town in Central Travancore on the way to his house. The backward castes were prohibited not only from entering the temple but also from traversing the temple road. The baron would alight from the car and take a side road to the end of the temple road while the upper caste driver would drive the car beyond the pollution notice board. The customary expensive life cycle rituals that would exhaust anyone's life savings in one's lifetime was an anachronism in the age of accumulation.

The traditional social structures and institutions such as matriliny and joint family, as well as extravagant customs connected to birth, marriage, and death ceremonies, etc., became impediments in the path of further progress. This was the background of the social reform movements that emerged in all castes and communities from the lowest to the highest from the latter half of the nineteenth century. The struggles conducted by the avarna[2] castes and communities for fundamental civil liberties, such as the right to dress according to one's fashion, carry umbrellas, wear ornaments, travel on public roads, worship in public temples, access to public education and employment, continued into the middle of the twentieth century. There were also numerous occasions of fairly widespread violent confrontations between the dominant castes and the aggrieved communities.

The Ezhava social reform movement was the most radical among them. The movement that was initiated as a religious reform campaign by Sree Narayana Guru later developed into a campaign for inter-dining and inter-marriage and even rationalism and atheism. Sree Narayana Guru became a source of legitimacy for Ezhava reformers and radicals of all hues and colours. The radicals transformed his sutra: 'One caste, one religion, and one God for man' into a new slogan: 'No caste, no religion and no God for man!' Such was the course of the development of radical democratic thought. The widespread dissemination of the radical interpretations of the Guru's teachings played an essential role in the emergence of the modern democratic consciousness in Kerala.

The Vaikom Temple Satyagraha agitation in 1924 became a significant turning point. At the initiative of Ezhava caste leaders like T.K. Madhavan, the Indian National Congress chose to sponsor the satyagraha struggle at Vaikom Temple. On Gandhiji's advice, the demand of the avarnas to enter the temples was scaled down to the right to walk through the roads adjacent to the temple. Despite Gandhiji's interventions and the nation-wide support to the struggle, after dragging on for nearly two years, it met with a subdued end. It created widespread disenchantment among

[2] The social groups outside the four varnas; avarnas are the oppressed social groups and have typically laboured for the savarnas.

Ezhavas about Gandhian tactics and his theories on Varnasrama Dharma (the caste hierarchy). As part of its national policy, the Congress withdrew from direct political activities in the princely states, creating a political vacuum in the state and a situation conducive for political fragmentation on communal lines.

Thus, when the constitutional reforms for 1932 were announced in Travancore, a national movement for 'responsible government' could not be launched despite the widespread awareness of the inadequacies of the reforms. The caste and community organisations in the Ezhava, Christian, and Muslim communities formed a Joint Political Congress demanding reservations in legislative representation and public employment. They started an Abstention Movement to boycott the elections conducted under the new constitution. The sweep of the struggle, as well as the threat of mass conversion of Ezhavas to Christianity, forced the administration to come to terms with the agitators. Communal reservations were guaranteed, and later public temples were thrown open to all Hindu castes.

The Congress nationalists generally denounced the Abstention Movement and its demands as sectarian. However, the CSP in Malabar, who argued for the active intervention of the Congress in the politics of princely states, extended support to the Abstention Movement despite its communal overtones. It correctly perceived the importance of linking the struggle against savarna[3] domination with the national movement. At the same time, the CSP strived to create mass and class organisations cutting across barriers of caste and community.

At the successful conclusion of the Abstention Movement, the leaders of the Joint Political Congress and savarna nationalists attempted to forge a common front — the Travancore State Congress — to fight for the 'responsible government'. The CSP warmly welcomed the move and attempted to rally the democratic

[3] The privileged social groups within the caste hierarchy that have controlled material resources and ritual practices.

sections under the banner of the State Congress. When the State Congress started a civil disobedience movement in August 1938, the Left KPCC came out in active support of the struggle by organizing solidarity *jathas*[4] to Travancore and setting up a Travancore Struggle Aid Committee across the border in Cochin.

E.M.S. Namboodiripad's emphasis on upper-caste domination as an essential feature of the traditional landlord system made caste reforms and struggle against caste a critical agenda of the Left, initially as part of the social reform movements and later from the independent platform of class organizations. This dialectical approach enabled the Left to attract the radical elements in the social reform movements to their ranks.

## THE GROWTH OF CLASS MOVEMENTS OF PEASANTS AND WORKERS

The credit for deciphering the true nature of the agrarian question in Malabar goes to E.M.S. Namboodiripad. Officially Malabar was a part of the Ryotwari settlement in the Madras presidency, where revenue settlement was made directly with the peasants. But in reality, the tenurial system of Malabar was dominated by absentee Brahmin landlords who leased the land to upper caste superior tenants who in turn leased it to lower caste tenants at will. Much of the actual cultivation was undertaken by agricultural labourers belonging to the lowest caste. Their situation was most deplorable with no security of tenure and without homesteads and burdened with exorbitantly high rent share and agricultural debts. The new understanding of the CSP changed the focus of the agrarian movement from the superior tenants to the mass of peasantry in Malabar, who were mostly inferior tenants and agricultural labourers.

Despite the global depression, the revenue settlement of 1929

[4] Jatha literally means a procession; it is a popular tactic in political rallies and social movements.

recommended a significant enhancement of the land tax. A new peasant movement centred around the poor peasantry developed in Malabar, demanding a reduction in rent and amending the Tenancy Act in favour of inferior tenants. In northern Malabar, notorious for feudal oppression, peasant upsurge was most widespread, militant, and violent. Starting with the campaign against illegal feudal exactions and oppressive social customs, the peasant movement in the region developed to the brink of a no rent campaign. The Congress Socialists were trying to build their Socialist Bardoli.[5]

The Congress Socialists transformed the existing philanthropic workers' association into militant trade unions and organized numerous new workers' organisations in all industrial centres. During the strike wave of 1935, the Congress Socialists took the initiative in organizing the first All Kerala Trade Union Conference at Calicut.[6] The emergence of workers as an independent class movement was a significant development that hastened the spread of communist ideology among the CSP ranks.

Unlike Malabar, a militant peasant movement did not develop in Travancore. The tenancy was not as widespread in the south as it was in Malabar. Therefore, the focus of CSP intervention in the southern regions was the industrial workers. Its most notable success was in Alleppey, the chief port town and centre of coir and oil industry of Travancore.

At the time of the entry of the CSP into Alleppey, the Travancore Labour Association had already transformed itself into a militant trade union under pressure from the ranks due to the severe deterioration of economic conditions.[7] However, despite the growth of a militant trade union movement on more significant issues of state and society, they were being led by caste and

[5] A reference to the Bardoli Satyagraha in Gujarat during the independence movement.

[6] Present-day Kozhikode.

[7] The discussion regarding the experience in Alappuzha is based on our analysis in Thomas Isaac (1985).

communal groups. The workers, most of whom were drawn from the Ezhava caste, were actively involved in the various anti-savarna movements, and were strongly influenced by the radical streams within them. We have documented in great detail, elsewhere, the process through which the dichotomy in the life of workers — as a member of a class at the workplace and as a member of a caste outside the workplace — came to be bridged and how the anti-savarna struggle became but one aspect of the general working-class struggle for democracy. It was made possible by the platform of the CSP that held the anti-savarna struggle to be a political task of the working class and active intervention on the basis of this platform.

The CSP sought to link up the rising tempo of working-class struggle at Alleppey to the agitation for 'responsible government' launched by the State Congress. An indefinite general strike was called with a charter of economic demands and, importantly, the political slogans of State Congress agitation at the end of 1938. However, the bourgeois leadership of the State Congress surrendered themselves before the administration and withdrew the agitation. The working class of Alleppey who had struck work in support of them held out steadfast in the path of struggle braving vicious repression let loose by the police and military. After holding out for a month, the workers returned to the factories. A new crop of class-conscious cadres, steeled in the struggle, rose to the movement's leadership, replacing the moderate leaders.

The determination of the Alleppey workers to continue their struggle against all odds won the admiration of the Youth Leaguers and the radical elements within the State Congress who were disillusioned by the vacillations of the leadership. The solidarity campaign started by these radical elements brought them in close contact with the working-class movement. This collaboration led to the formation of the Radical Group in May 1939, with M.N. Govindan Nair as the secretary. The Radical Group was to function as an organised socialist faction within the State Congress on the lines of the CSP in Malabar. The members of the Radical Group, except for a small faction led by N. Sreekantan Nair, became the leading core of the CPI in Travancore in 1940.

## THE SECOND WORLD WAR AND THE CPI IN KERALA

During the first phase of the War, the CPI adopted a line of unconditional resistance to the imperialist war. The consequent police repression and preventive detention of cadres and the fact that the CPI was an illegal party forced the young communists in Kerala to adopt underground organisational forms and new styles of mass work. Thus, the first phase of the War rapidly transformed the loose and open organisational structure of the CSP into a communist party of *steel discipline* (a phrase that gained wide currency in Malayalam).

After the German aggression against the Soviet Union, the CPI's tactics changed. The transition from unconditional opposition to unconditional support to the war efforts was a painful adjustment. While there was no doubt in the mind of any communist on the need to rally to the defence of international socialism, there was much confusion as to how to link up this international task with the struggle for national liberation. The party failed to take into account the patriotic motives of the masses and leaders in the Quit India Movement while evolving tactics to oppose their disruption.

All this is not to suggest that the tactics of the opposition to the Quit India movement did not create any adverse long-term consequences. It created for the first time a generation of Leftists in Kerala who were anti-Communists. Another development with equally far-reaching consequences was the splintering of the mass movements. To counter the mass influence of the Communists, Congress pursued a policy of splitting the existing mass organisations or setting up rival ones.

There was also temporary isolation from a good section of the nationalist masses which was indeed a matter of deep concern and frustration within the party cadres who had just emerged from the ranks of Congress Socialism. However, the wild accusations of the Congress leaders about the communists being the agents of the British and so on were never taken seriously. Kerala communists possessed one great asset: they were the leaders of the national movement in Kerala.

Despite these challenges, for the CPI, this war period saw an increase in the party membership, the membership of the mass organisations, the sales of party literature, the circulation of the party journal *Deshabhimani*, the response to the fund collection drives, and so on. The party successfully consolidated its influence and made significant inroads, especially in southern Kerala. Several factors contributed to the success of the CPI during this phase of its growth.

An important factor was that it was not subdued with the 'production disease' of the war period that had infected the party in India. Though the production policy constituted the main link in kisan and trade union fronts, the cadres exhibited extraordinary skill, especially in working-class centres like Alleppey, in adopting tactics that ensured the fulfilment of day-to-day demands of the masses without taking recourse to forms of struggles that would have disrupted the war efforts seriously.

The communists were at the forefront of every activity that could relieve the distress caused by the war, such as famine, scarcity of necessities such as cloth and kerosene, the outbreak of epidemics, natural calamities, etc. Since Kerala was a chronically grain deficit region, the disruption of supply routes due to the hostilities created near-famine conditions. The CPI worked out concrete proposals for the procurement of grain stocks and statutory rationing and organised mass campaigns for their implementation. When rationing was introduced, the party again came to the forefront to expose its inefficiencies and agitate for remedial measures. The party's relief work also won widespread admiration.

## THE POST-WAR REVOLUTIONARY UPSURGE AND THE PUNNAPRA–VAYALAR UPRISING

It was only by the middle of 1946 that the CPI national leadership realized the sweep of the post-war upsurge in struggles as evidenced from Tebhaga, Worli, Telangana, and the RIN Mutiny, and worked out the main slogans of developing the partial struggles for the achievement of democratic revolution and seizure of power by the people. In August 1946, the Central Committee of the CPI called on the party to develop them into 'local battles' and 'raise the question of state power'.

The new line was reflected in the upsurge of struggles in Kerala. In Malabar, the CPI's main thrust was in the agrarian sector — the campaign against hoarders and forcible occupation of wastelands — which led to violent confrontations, such as Karivallur and Kavumbai.[8] However, the major battle was the Punnapra-Vayalar struggle (named after the two main centres on confrontation near Alleppey in Travancore). This struggle was one of the rare events in the history of the Indian working-class movement when the industrial workers not only programmatically but also physically led an armed movement of the rural masses.

The relatively higher incidence of landlordism and feudal vestiges in the region compared to the other parts of Travancore, the tyrannical overlordship of the traditional communal elite over the poor fishermen of the catholic community, the famine

[8] Karivallur and Kavumbai: These were prominent sites of peasant action in the Malabar region. Conditions of acute starvation and famine were common, while paddy was routinely hoarded and smuggled to black markets by the landlords in collusion with the state machinery, primarily the Malabar State Police (MSP). In Karivallur, on 20 December 1946, when villagers resisted this practice, the police opened fire and those leading the resistance fell to police bullets and hundreds of others were arrested. In Kavumbai, another village, with a long tradition of resistance, Communist Party leaders along with villagers, decided to raid the villagers' godowns. The landlords sought police help and four comrades were martyred, while hundreds were arrested and tortured.

conditions, and acute unemployment cumulatively/collectively provided fertile soil for the fast development of the revolutionary movement in the countryside. Threatened by the unrest, the rural reaction attempted to terrorise the workers into submission. The workers retaliated sporadically initially and later in a more organised manner. In the first week of September 1946, this led to the entry of the military into the area to meet the 'communist menace'. With the approach of the harvest season, the tensions and repression escalated, forcing the terror-stricken workers in many localities to flee from their homesteads to areas where the movement was more robust and to set up camps for self-protection.

The party leadership in Travancore, closely following the CPI's new tactical line, tried to link the fierce partial struggles in the Alleppey countryside with the general political struggles for a final onslaught on the feudal monarchy. A mass agitation on the scale of 1938 was envisaged. However, unlike in 1938, the organised working class, through a general strike all over Travancore, was to spearhead the struggle. The self-defence camps developed in the Alleppey countryside were sought to be transformed into volunteer camps where the workers were to be given training in close physical combat and military manoeuvres.

The general strike began on 22 October. It was evident from the beginning that the strategy had failed. Not only did the State Congress not support the agitation, as the liberal national leaders had promised, but a section of them came out openly against the uprising. Thus, the state-wide mass agitation never materialised. Even the general strike was a complete success only in Alleppey as the non-communist Left developed cold feet at the last moment. Thus, the Alleppey workers were isolated. Martial law was declared in the region, and the military reinforcements moved into Alleppey. In the large-scale military operations mounted against the volunteer camps, around 500 cadres and people were gunned down or tortured to death. Despite the self-sacrificing heroism and the political determination of the workers, resistance was ruthlessly suppressed in less than a week.

The crucial flaw was the failure to ensure a state-wide agitation as in 1938. The optimism regarding the development of the mass agitation sprang from the CPI's illusions about a significant section of the State Congress leaders joining the struggle. The party also overestimated its preparedness to organize such a moment. The tactics adopted in the struggle closely corresponded to the 'general strike and mass insurrection model' and ignored the need for mobility and partisan warfare.

The Punnapra-Vayalar uprising was the peak point of the national movement in Kerala. It sealed the fate of the monarchy in Travancore. More importantly, it signified the maturing of the working class that had emerged as an independent political force in 1938 into the leadership of the national movement in 1946. This status and prestige that the Communists gained through militant struggles, particularly in North Malabar and Punnapra-Vayalar on the eve of the independence, was an important factor that facilitated the rapid spread of the CPI in the 'fifties.

## MOVEMENT FOR UNITED KERALA

In a sense the Punnapra-Vayalar uprising was a blow against separatism and in favour of national unity. A united Kerala of Malayalam-speaking population within the Indian Union was the interpretation of the national question. The CPI, which had already brought the three regions of Malabar, Cochin and Travancore under a unified regional political leadership and an all-Kerala trade union movement, put forward as a practical slogan the formation of a United Kerala consisting of the Malayalam speaking areas in the above three regions. The struggle for United Kerala was to be an inseparable part of the struggle of the people for national freedom and the liquidation of feudal monarchies.

The perspective of the CPI enabled it to ride on the crest of the wave of Malayali national feeling as well as a cultural movement in the post-war years. Almost every well-known literary figure or artist was either a Communist activist or sympathiser at one time or other. Libraries and reading rooms mushroomed. Art and literature were widely used not merely for propaganda but were viewed as harbingers of new earth and heaven.

The Communist Party was banned and remained so even during the 1952 Parliament elections in Travancore–Cochin. Still, it was able to win two seats. The CPI's vote share was less than 10 per cent. But the prestige of the Party as the leader of the national movement, organiser of trade unions and peasant associations, close links with the radical elements in the caste movements and radical hegemony in the cultural arena held out much larger promise than its low vote share. In 1956, in the first State Assembly elections in the newly formed state of Kerala, the Communist Party secured 40 per cent of the votes, and along with its independents, it won a narrow majority.

Chapter 3

# The First Communist Ministry (1957–59) and Afterwards: Growth and Stalemate of Left Influence

The victory of the Communists in the 1957 assembly election took everyone, both friends and foes, by surprise. It was in Andhra that the Communists had expected their first electoral victory, helped by tail winds of the Telangana armed struggle. However, Congress sensing a possible election setback, succeeded in forging a broad united front, including with the other political parties. The imminent threat of a Communist victory polarised the voters in favour of the Congress. Though CPI won 40 per cent of the votes in Andhra, it could gain only 8 per cent of the seats.

Learning the lessons from the Andhra debacle, the CPI in Kerala did not make any tall claims and announced as its aim the formation of a united front government with the other Left parties. However, the other Left parties decided to fight on their own, and the CPI had to be content with supporting several prominent independents. Even CPI General Secretary Ajay Ghosh publicly refused to claim a victory in Kerala. The Congress, overwhelmed with self-confidence, let its guard down and did not heed the advice of the church to forge an anti-Communist United Front.

The CPI received 40 per cent of the votes and 60 Party MLAs and five independents in the 127 members assembly. It had a majority of 3 seats. The governor insisted on interviewing each of the independents in a last-minute move to thwart the formation of a Communist ministry. Finally, on 5 April 1957, an 11-member ministry led by E.M.S. Namboodiripad, as Chief Minister, was sworn in. It was a galaxy of eminent Malayalees such as Joseph Mundaserry, the foremost literary critic, Dr K.B. Menon, well known medical practitioner Krishna Iyer, one of the leading jurists, as well as stalwarts of the Communist Party such as C. Achuthamenon, K.R. Gowri, T.V. Thomas, and K.C. George who would continue to play key roles in Kerala politics.

## THE AGENDA FOR UNITED KERALA

The CPI was fully prepared for taking on the mantle of power: it was the only party that had presented a Manifesto before the people. At a special convention held in 1956 at Thrissur, on the eve of state formation, it had adopted a comprehensive document on the development of a United Kerala. A decade back, EMS had set the ball rolling with his book *Kerala, the Motherland of Malayalees*, which traced historically the evolution of the economy, society, and culture of Malayalees and briefly outlined the potential of a United Kerala within independent India. Therefore, the new government started to implement an agenda leaving no sector untouched and would continue to influence the future course of development of Kerala right from the word go (Namboodiripad, 1948).

The first major order of the new government was to ban all evictions of tenants. It was followed by debt relief, abolition of non-rent payments to landlords and compensation payment to tenants for their land improvement and finally, in the first year itself, a comprehensive agrarian bill. The bill reduced sharply the rent to be paid by the tenant who could not in any case be evicted. The tenant could become the full owner of the land by paying a multiple of the fair rent so fixed. All hutment tenants were to be given ownership of the hutment land. A low-ceiling on-land holdings was to be introduced. An over-the-envelope calculation showed that the surplus land would be sufficient for the distribution of cultivable land for the landless. The law was passed and sent to the President of India, who kept it in abeyance without giving consent. The plan to nationalise foreign plantations had to be shelved as presidential assent would surely have been denied. The upper caste community organisations, particularly the Nair Service Society (NSS), which was ruffled by the growing stature of the Christian elite, had tacitly refused to join with the anti-Communist rhetoric during the elections; it felt threatened and protested. But all efforts to dilute the provisions of the law were rejected (Lieten,1982; Sreekala, 2007).

The new ministry encouraged collective bargaining. The labour department was strengthened, tripartite committees formed, and the police was prohibited from interfering in labour disputes. According to the new police policy, they could intervene only in case of a law-and-order problem. Lock-up torture was prohibited. The new policy gave a fillip to the trade union movement and for the improvement of wages. Minimum wages were fixed for agricultural labourers.

A comprehensive education bill was introduced in the State Assembly to achieve universal and compulsory education within ten years. Free food and uniforms were to be supplied to the students. The bill provided security and uniform emoluments to the teachers and social control in the selection process for government-aided private institutions. The law also envisaged local popular education councils. The latter two proposals infuriated the powerful private management lobby, particularly the main stakeholder, the catholic church. It was as if their worst fears of a communist takeover were coming true. Protests and agitations started but did not gain momentum.

The 1957 ministry was also a landmark for the spread of education and health facilities to northern Kerala, which lagged behind Travancore–Cochin. Kerala University was established, and Prof John Mathai, a former member of Nehru's cabinet, was selected as the first Vice-Chancellor. Malayalam was declared as the medium of governance and education. Cultural academies were formed.

The major initiative in the infrastructure sector was the preparation of two master plans, one for water resources and the other for electricity development. While the government was committed to the public sector and demanded higher central public sector investment, it also encouraged private investment. The agreement with Birla to establish a rayons factory in Kozhikkode raised eyebrows all-around at that time.

An Administrative Reforms Committee, headed by the Chief Minister, prepared a roadmap for transforming the government machinery inherited from the colonial era. Based on the recommendations of the committee, a comprehensive bill for decentralising governance was introduced. It put forward the vision of a district government with development and regulatory functions, besides autonomous panchayats and municipalities.

The finance minister C. Achuthamenon, one of the future Chief Ministers of Kerala, had a Camelot of young radical advisors, including Ashok Mitra, I.S. Gulati, Satyabratha Sen and Ashok Rudra, to prepare the budget and formulate fiscal policy. The fiscal stance was in favour of increased social expenditure. However, the revenue deficit was to be kept in check by higher resource mobilisation. Public borrowing, including the sale of sterling bonds inherited from the Travancore government, was used to finance capital expenditure. The neglect of Kerala by the Central Government was criticised. Young I.S. Gulati, in a series of articles in *Economic Weekly* titled 'Behind the Coir Curtain', chronicled some of the excitement of the period.

## THE ANTI-COMMUNIST LIBERATION STRUGGLE

The initial agitation related to land reforms and education policy seemed to be subsiding, and by all indications, popular support for the government was growing. In a bye-election in the plantation area, with predominantly Tamil voters, the Left won a resounding victory. But all of a sudden, at the beginning of 1959, foreboding dark political clouds began to gather, and the state was pushed into the vortex of a virulent anti-Communist agitation, styled as the 'Liberations Struggle'. A close reading of the political events so far does not indicate the explosion that occurred in June–July 1959. It was not a struggle that gathered strength step-by-step into a hurricane but more in the nature of a well-planned coup.[1]

The church took the initiative to forge an all-in united front of community organisations and political parties against the so-called Communist cell rule. Even the non-Communist Left political parties were roped in. There was a blitzkrieg of ideological propaganda against communism, with wild allegations of nationalisation of all private property, destruction of the family, and women being made common property. The intensity of the propaganda from church pulpits to political mass meetings, newspapers joining the chorus, the utilisation of art performance and literature, transformed the popular psyche in a matter of few months – something closely paralleling the Guatemalan agitation against the elected Left government of Jacob Arbenz in Guatemala in 1954.

With the Communist government refusing to yield, demands began to be raised for central interventions to dismiss the government on the grounds of the breakdown of law and order. The demand was similar to the one raised against the Left government of Cheddi Jagan in British Guyana by the agitationists in 1953. Masses of people, mostly women and children, were mobilised around churches and undertook picketing and demonstrations leading to violence and police actions. The police actions, including killing people in firing, only further fanned up the agitation and resulted in the breakdown of law and order. It was a perfect alibi for the central government headed by Nehru, who initially was opposed to central intervention and would not find fault with the communist government's legislations, to dismiss it on 31 July 1959.

The agitation against the Communist government was evidently a part of the destabilisation program that the US government

[1] The discussion of anti-communist Liberation Struggle is based on Thomas Isaac (2008).

launched against a number of democratically elected communist or Left governments that came to power in the three continents during the post-World War period. It included Guatemala, British Guyana, Iran, Congo, Brazil, Chile, and Indonesia. The CIA and the US government documents of all these successful US operations are available in plenty in public and studied by numerous scholars today. But the Kerala episode still remains clouded in mystery though more and more documents related to it are being released by US authorities which reveal US apprehensions of Communist victory, their close monitoring of events at the highest level, and coordination with Indian intelligence. Two US ambassadors, Ellsworth Bunker and Daniel Patrick Moynihan, have testified to the US financing of the agitation.

Perhaps, the presence of a very powerful, articulate, and organised anti-Communist platform in Kerala headed by the church did not make it necessary to have any direct intervention of US agencies as in Latin America and Africa. An influential anti-Communist media also existed in Kerala and did not have to be invented. Further, Nehru would not have tolerated any direct interference, and therefore the dealings of the CIA with Indian intelligence had to be discreet. Even the debriefing circulars insisted on complete secrecy. CIA interventions continued through to the 1961 elections even after the dismissal of the government.

The abrupt end to the first government in Kerala left an unfinished agenda. It continued to influence the future course of development but was a major missed opportunity. For example, it took more than a decade before the next Left government could implement comprehensive land reforms. By this time, most of the surplus lands were subdivided or sold away by the landlords, and there was not much surplus land that the government could take over. This became the Achilles' heel of the land reforms, denying cultivable land to scheduled castes and landless agricultural workers. The private-aided education sector has ever since remained an unresolved thorny issue. It took more than four decades before the state could implement a successful democratic decentralisation. The false propaganda of Communist anarchy and violence created a mental block to investors to come to Kerala even though Kerala has been below the national average for the last four decades by all indicators of industrial strikes.

## THE LEFT GOVERNMENT 1967–69

The formation of the Communist government in Kerala also intensified the internal debate within the CPI on the potential and limitations of transitional state governments. Would the formation of more similar state governments lead to a peaceful transformation to socialism? Those who believed that this was not possible pointed to the limitations of such governments and the experience of Kerala, where the reactionaries and the central government did not permit even a moderate progressive reform agenda. The differences in the CPI were related to the question of how to assess the nature of the Congress and the policies of the Congress government. The Nehru government's development policy emphasised import substitution, the public sector, and planning. In the realm of foreign policy, it refused to join the US camp, championed non-alignment, and was friendly with the Soviet Union. Therefore, a section in the CPI wanted to collaborate with Congress. The Left-wing fiercely opposed such a strategy. The accentuation of this conflict finally led to a split in the Communist Party and the creation of two parties, one the CPI and the other CPI(Marxist). The CPI(M) with its militant slogans and charismatic EMS and AKG in the leadership earned the loyalty of the vast majority of members and sympathisers in Kerala, as was demonstrated in the 1965 state assembly election.

The anti-Communist front that had come to power in 1961 broke up, and its government came to an end by 1964. In the 1965 election, all parties fought separately, including CPI and CPI(M). Many of the CPI(M) candidates fought the election from jail because of their political stand during the 1962 India–China conflict. The Party had a limited tacit understanding with the Muslim League in some constituencies. The results produced a hung assembly, with the CPI(M) winning 40 seats and being the largest party. The governor refused to give the CPI(M) a chance to form the government, and president's rule was imposed.

In the 1967 election, a seven-party united front led by CPI(M) won a thumping victory. Kerala was not an isolated instance. In West Bengal, another state with a dominant Left presence, a government was formed with Left participation. Regional parties formed non-Congress governments in many of the other states. The majority of the people were under non-Congress state governments. The trend of Left parties and regional parties to be the dominant rival political formation to Congress, in terms of the number of parliament and legislative assembly members vis-a-vis the right-wing parties, reached its peak in 1967. The Left was leading the alternative to the Congress. The rising tide of peasant struggles for land and trade union strikes boosted the Left alternative. It appeared that a major political crisis was brewing and that the role of Left state governments had to be defined in this concrete context. The Left state governments were to be instruments of struggle and, at best, could provide immediate relief to the people.

This understanding of the CPI(M) was in conflict with the CPI, who, even as participants in the Left governments in Kerala and West Bengal, stuck to their programmatic understanding of collaboration with Congress. The continuous bickering and polemics finally ended in the disruption of the Left governments. In Kerala, the major non-CPI(M) coalition partners formed a new government with the outside support of Congress. Later a coalition of non-CPI(M) parties, including the Congress, won the elections and formed the government.

The latter half of the 1970s proved to be a turning point in national politics. By then, the revolutionary up tide of the 1960s had exhausted itself mainly due to the splits in the broad Left coalition. The socialists adopted a strategy of an all-in-one united front with the right-wing forces to defeat the Congress. The CPI moved into a phase of collaboration with Congress. The CPI(M) was brutally suppressed with semi-fascist terror in West Bengal. It also suffered a split with the Left extremist faction that sided with China and wanted to launch armed warfare against the Indian government. The CPI(M) ploughed a lonely furlough, rejecting the propositions of both the Soviets and the Chinese and seeking to combine parliamentary and extra-parliamentary struggles against the Indian government led by the Congress party. Cornered by mass agitation against corruption and adverse stricture by the court, the Congress resorted to draconian measures, including the declaration of a national emergency. Since then, national politics entered a new phase of right-wing ascendancy. However, in Kerala, it proved to be the beginning of a new phase where the Left forces joined together to form periodically non-Congress governments.

## THE LEFT GOVERNMENTS OF 1980, 1987, 1996, 2006, AND 2016

The 1980 Left government led by E.K. Nayanar was a broad coalition of all who were opposed to the authoritarian trends in the Congress, including a major Congress faction led by A.K. Antony. This government did not complete its second year since A.K. Antony and his followers, along with the Kerala Congress, withdrew from the government. Since then, Kerala politics has revolved around the Left Democratic Front (LDF), consisting of both the Communist parties and other secular non-Congress parties, and the United Democratic Front (UDF), consisting of the Congress, Muslim League, Kerala Congress, and various community-based anti-Communist groups.

The Left governments that came to power in the following

decades have contributed significantly to the development of the state, each with its own innovative development programmes to its credit. The 1987 Left government led by E.K. Nayanar successfully launched a mass movement for the Total Literacy Program. This experience led to the formation of the National Literacy Mission. The 1996 Left government, led once again by E.K. Nayanar, launched the People's Plan Campaign, one of the most radical devolution programs undertaken anywhere in the world. The 2006 Left government led by V.S. Achuthanandan was remarkable for its rejuvenation of the public sector enterprises and its anti-recession stimulus package. The remarkable success of the 2016 Left government led by Pinarayi Vijayan and its subsequent victory in the 2021 election has been the inspiration for the current book.

All Left governments have been noted for their welfare and social programs. However, we can discern a slow shift from the understanding of 1967 towards policies focused on possibilities of regional development and framing of alternative development policies within the federal system, which will be elaborated in the later chapters.

## STAGNATION OF THE ELECTORAL BASE OF THE LEFT

Despite the innovative programs and relatively better performance of the Left governments, the electoral support base of the Left tended to stagnate. In Table 3.1, we present the vote share of LDF, UDF, and NDA or its earlier communal formations in all the elections to the state assembly, parliament, and local governments since 1987. The constituents of the three fronts have been broadly the same.

It is very evident that after a meteoric expansion of the support base in the 1950s, the Left expansion has plateaued off. In the assembly elections, the vote share of the LDF ranged between 48.63 in 2006 and 43.35 in 2016. In the parliament elections, its vote share ranged between 46.23 in 2009 to 35.10 in 2019. In local government elections, it ranged between 41.91 in 2015 and 49.22 in 2005. The average vote share for the LDF during the past three and half decades has fluctuated around 45 per cent, and that of UDF has fluctuated around 44 per cent.

As a result, a victory of either of the two fronts would depend on a swing of two or three per cent either way. Given the highly rights conscious electorate, the anti-incumbency factor alone would be sufficient to result in the defeat of the ruling front. It was as if the politics in Kerala were fossilised between the UDF and the LDF, with their popular support roughly equal.

In the parliament elections, but for the exceptional case in 2004, the UDF has consistently earned a higher vote share than the LDF. In 9 parliament elections, the LDF vote share averaged 42.67 per cent and that of UDF averaged 45.63. The electorate does not perceive the Left to come to power at the Centre and therefore, a section shifts to UDF for parliamentary elections.

In contrast, the Left, with a better grass root level network, has an advantage in the local government elections. In the six local government elections, the average LDF vote share has been 43.92 per cent, and that of the UDF has been 41.37 per cent. The vote share of independents and others is around 3 per cent in the assembly and parliament elections, while it is nearly 6 per cent in the local government elections.

The key question remains: Why has the Left not been able to create a breakthrough and achieve a decisive majority above 50 per cent of the electorate. The answer is not easy. All that we would propose here is that it should not be reduced to the ability of individual leaders, the capacity of the organisation or such other accidental or subjective factors. There are certain objective factors related to social structure and production relations that impeded the advance of the Left. We shall briefly identify these impediments.

**Table 3.1 The percentage vote share of LDF, UDF and NDA 1987–2021**

| Election | LDF | UDF | NDA |
|---|---|---|---|
| 1987 Assembly | 44.96 | 44.29 | 6.47 |
| 1989 Parliament | 44.15 | 48.99 | 4.48 |
| 1991 Assembly | 45.93 | 48.14 | 4.74 |
| 1991 Parliament | 44.29 | 48.60 | 3.85 |
| 1995 Local Government | 44.70 | 42.85 | 6.11 |
| 1996 Assembly | 44.01 | 44.76 | 6.08 |
| 1996 Parliament | 44.22 | 44.97 | 5.92 |
| 1998 Parliament | 44.31 | 45.64 | 7.91 |
| 1999 Parliament | 43.60 | 46.89 | 8.01 |
| 2000 Local Government | 42.64 | 41.48 | 5.83 |
| 2001 Assembly | 43.70 | 49.17 | 5.20 |
| 2004 Parliament | 46.23 | 38.45 | 12.1 |
| 2005 Local Government | 49.22 | 40.21 | 5.42 |
| 2006 Assembly | 48.63 | 42.98 | 4.75 |
| 2009 Parliament | 41.95 | 47.82 | 6.49 |
| 2010 Local Government | 42.46 | 46.08 | 6.17 |
| 2011 Assembly | 45.13 | 46.03 | 6.08 |
| 2014 Parliament | 40.20 | 42.04 | 10.83 |
| 2015 Local Government | 41.91 | 40.26 | 14.23 |
| 2016 Assembly | 43.35 | 38.79 | 15.01 |
| 2019 Parliament | 35.10 | 47.23 | 15.56 |
| 2020 Local Government | 42.57 | 37.32 | 14.94 |
| 2021 Assembly | 45.28 | 39.40 | 12.49 |

Source: Election statistics prepared by AKG Centre for Research and Studies, Thiruvananthapuram.

## THE CASTE AND COMMUNITY STRUCTURE OF KERALA

The most important issue is related to the caste and community structure of Kerala's society. A large proportion of Kerala's society is from India's minority communities: 27 per cent Muslims and 18 per cent Christians. The Hindu community is divided by castes, with around 17 per cent upper castes, 28 per cent backward castes, and 10 per cent scheduled castes and tribes. The social reform movements that we discussed in the last chapter had a greater impact on the Hindu community, particularly amongst the backward castes. It is in the soil upturned by these renaissance movements that the seeds of Left radicalism came to flourish. As can be seen from Table 3.2, the vote share of the Left is highest among scheduled castes (63 per cent) and then among backward castes, particularly Ezhavas (53 per cent), and relatively low among Nairs and other upper castes (34 per cent). Overall, the Left vote share in the Hindu community is around 49 per cent.

In contrast, the Left influence among the minorities has been relatively much lower at around 29 per cent among the Christians and 31 per cent among Muslims. It is also seen that, but for the Dalits, the vote share of all other communities in the parliament election for the Left is lower than those in the assembly elections for the Left.

The catholic church from the late 1930s built a very powerful anti-Communist lobby and was hostile to the radical movements. Nevertheless, a number of early leaders of the CPI in Travancore–Cochin hailed from the Christian community, starting from K.V. Pathrose, the first secretary of the CPI in Travancore, K.C. George, who succeeded him, and T.V. Thomas, the most well-known Communist face in Southern Kerala. The anti-Communist liberation of 1959 struggle proved to be the turning point, with the church whipping up anti-Communist religious hysteria and ostracising the communists from the community. It foreclosed the flow of cadres to the party from the Christian community until the latter half of the 1970s, when a new generation of student leaders rose to prominence. The liberation theology streams were relatively weak within the Kerala church. The efforts for a Christian–Marxist dialogue proved to be ineffective. Political alliances with Kerala Congress factions, dominated by the Christian farmers and the church, were also experimented with by the Left.

As noted earlier, with the repression of the Mappila rebellion of 1921, the Muslim community in Kerala turned away even from the

**Table 3.2 The vote share of LDF, UDF and NDA in different communities**

| Community | Front | Average of 4 Parliament elections from 2004 to 2019 | Average of 4 Assembly elections from 2006 to 2021 | Average of Parliament and Assembly elections |
|---|---|---|---|---|
| Nair | LDF | 27.50 | 41.50 | 34.50 |
| | UDF | 32.25 | 34.75 | 33.50 |
| | BJP | 29.75 | 20.75 | 25.25 |
| Ezhava | LDF | 49.00 | 57.75 | 53.38 |
| | UDF | 26.75 | 25.50 | 26.13 |
| | BJP | 16.00 | 13.50 | 14.75 |
| Muslim | LDF | 27.50 | 34.50 | 31.00 |
| | UDF | 62.25 | 59.50 | 60.88 |
| | BJP | 2.00 | 1.50 | 1.75 |
| Christian | LDF | 27.00 | 32.00 | 29.50 |
| | UDF | 66.25 | 60.50 | 63.38 |
| | BJP | 2.30 | 3.50 | 2.90 |
| Dalits | LDF | 63.50 | 63.33 | 63.42 |
| | UDF | 22.75 | 20.00 | 21.38 |
| | BJP | 12.00 | 14.33 | 13.17 |

Source: CSDS–Lokniti Survey as reported in *The Hindu* (May 6, 2021), *Indian Express* (March 20, 2021) and CSDS Team with G. Gopakumar (2004).

liberal ideological streams. Nevertheless, the relationship with the nascent Left in Malabar was warm because the latter did not share the apprehensions of upper caste leaders of the national movement regarding the Muslim community and Muslim political action. However, the Muslim League joined the anti-Communist united front in 1957. By 1967 the anti-Communist front completely broke up, and the Left united front, which included the Muslim League, came to power. With the downfall of the government, the League joined the Congress front and has shared power in every UDF government in Kerala since then.

A split away from the League styled as the All-India Muslim League joined the LDF. However, it was realised by the Left leadership that the tactics of aligning with a Muslim political party were not helping the Left in advancing its direct influence among the Muslim community. On the other hand, the League's influence was strengthening and spread to Southern Kerala. The review of tactics of alliance with Muslim parties became a subject matter of serious inner-party strife within the CPI(M) and was finally clinched by ousting the faction that vehemently stuck to the alliance. Since then, the LDF has not had any faction of the League in its fold. Against the popular perception of a weakened LDF due to the exit of the League faction from the front, the Left won a resounding victory in the 1987 election. Though its influence in the Muslim community has tended to improve, it continued to remain at a relatively lower level.

## THE AGRARIAN QUESTION IN THE POST LAND REFORM PERIOD

Another major impediment to the Left advance was the complexity of the agrarian question in the post-land reform era. Land reform in Kerala did not result in a substantial increase in productivity or production due to a host of reasons. The absence of a complementary package of land and water management, agricultural inputs, agro-processing, and credit was the most important reason. How this situation weakened the efforts of the Left in agrarian mobilisation during the post-land reform period is summarised below.

First, Kerala agriculture was characterised by small holdings, the average size of the holding in the non-plantation sector being around 20 cents. Some people have criticised the land reform for fragmentation of land holdings. It may be noted that land reforms, only brought about a change in ownership and not the size of the operational holding. The fragmentation is essentially a result of population pressure and changes in the inheritance system.

Normally the small size of holdings need not result in a decline in productivity as the size productivity inverse relationship debate in India exemplifies. The small holders, without alternative recourse to subsistence, would attempt to maximize the total production in the small holding. This was not to be in Kerala, because, unlike in the rest of India, the small holders were also heavily dependent on wage labourers. The nature of Kerala's settlement and occupation pattern is rooted in a rural-urban continuum. Because the income from small holdings is insufficient for livelihood and because there are alternative non-agricultural occupations in the countryside, the small holders get engaged in more remunerative non-agricultural jobs. Though they are not landlords, they are dependent on wage labourers for agricultural operations. Therefore, they maximize production only subject to marginal productivity cost considerations.

Second, the social security provided by ownership of hutment land that derived from the land reforms and the rapid spread of agricultural workers' unions increased their bargaining power and resulted in the escalation of wage rates. The large-scale migration to the Gulf countries by construction and other unskilled labourers led to the wage increase in these sectors and generated pressures on wage rates in non-migrant sectors, including agriculture. Rapid increases in wage rates without proportional change in productivity led to a shift in cropping patterns in favour of less labour-intensive tree crops. The farmers began to reduce labour-intensive operations and gave up inter-crops leading to a sharp decline in the cropping intensity of homestead gardens. More and more paddy lands were left fallow.

Third, the above process adversely affected agriculture income. Cultivation became more and more unremunerative. However, the landholders clung to their land even though the income from cultivation was meagre because of the capital gains generated by the rapid increase in land prices. Land was an important asset for investment by the migrants resulting in a boom in the land market and prices. With astronomically high land prices, no one would purchase land as an agricultural investment or, in other words, high land prices acted as a new version of Marx's rent barrier concept (Karl Marx, *Capital III*).

Fourth, the escalation of land prices led to widespread illegal reclamation of paddy lands and wetlands into garden lands. With paddy lands lying fallow, the traditional water regulation systems in the paddy valleys fell into disuse and became non-functional. The spread of tree crops and forest encroachment in the hill tracks resulted in denudation and less water carrying capacity of the catchment areas. The net result of these trends was disruption of the traditional water cycle of Kerala; the state, with one of the highest rainfalls, began to witness drought in summer and flood in monsoon. There is no doubt that the lack of scientific land and water management was a major factor contributing to the agrarian crisis.

Fifth, the conflict between the farmers and the agricultural labourers in the context of wage escalation and stagnant productivity was attempted to be resolved through a united struggle for higher prices. This response was effective until the neoliberal measures initiated during the 1990s. The external terms of trade were favourable to Kerala. The situation rapidly changed with the removal of import barriers, particularly through the ASEAN Free Trade Treaty. The end of the 1990s witnessed a collapse of the prices of almost all the commercial crops in the state, and Kerala was engulfed in a major crisis.

The unprecedented crisis in the economy and consequently in government finances resulted in the electoral defeat of the Left in the 2001 elections to the assembly despite the remarkable achievements of the democratic decentralisation popular movement that we shall discuss in chapter 5.

The nature of the agrarian question in Kerala during the post-land reform phase has been a theoretical issue that has been debated in Left circles and described in resolutions adopted by the CPI(M) and the peasant movement. We have attempted to summarise the important trends in these documents in the paragraphs above. The improvement in productivity is important not only for an increase in agricultural income but also for the unity of farmers and agricultural workers. One of the objectives of radical devolution was precisely to address the issue of stagnation in agricultural production through participatory planning and bringing together the entire local agricultural community.

## THE NEW MIDDLE CLASS

We may also mention the broad social stratification in Kerala in the post-land reform period. Redistribution of land, rise in wages and social security measures adopted by the government softened the polarisation and contributed to the emergence of a growing middle class. Education with reservation to government jobs also enabled lower strata upward mobility. Migration and inflow of remittances was yet another factor that contributed to greater social mobility. The growth of the new middle class accelerated under the neoliberal regime. In contrast to the broad experience of Kerala during the post-independence period, inequality between the households, rural and urban areas, agriculture, and non-agriculture sectors and between the districts in Kerala began to widen from the 1990s. Today we may say that the new middle class would constitute the top two deciles of the households. And another 40 per cent of the population aspire to join this new middle class.

Kerala has been undergoing rapid urbanization. The new middle class is predominantly urban in nature. This class is very different from the middle class that had been at the forefront of the social reform movements and behind the radical stirrings in the past. The new elite is not satisfied with the education and health facilities built up through the past decades. Their aspiration levels are much higher, and they increasingly withdrew from the social support for the traditional social infrastructure. The educated generation was no longer satisfied with handicraft jobs but demanded quality jobs more in tune with their educational qualifications.

Ideologically they gravitated towards neoliberal logic and became key elements contributing to a rightward shift in politics. They became active participants in the revival of caste and community organisations which, unlike in the past, were shorn of any radicalism but inherited only the caste shells of the old social reform movements. This middle class in the Hindu community has also been the main contributor to the rise of the Hindutva movement in the state. With a large segment of Kerala population under the delusion of joining the ranks of the middle class, it was very important that the Left, whose main mass base consists of the bottom poor, develop a program to build a bridge to the growing middle class.

How the Left has attempted to address the above three challenges during the last quarter of a century is the theme of discussion in the subsequent chapters.

Chapter 4

# The Redistributive Development Strategy and Making of the Kerala Model

Having traced the growth of the Communist movement in Kerala, we shall now examine how it has impacted the fashioning of a redistributive development strategy in the state. Such a strategy would necessarily have three key elements:

1. First, redistribution of income from higher wages through collective bargaining.
2. Second, redistribution of assets through land reforms.
3. Third, guaranteed basic services through public provisioning of healthcare, education, and other services.

More recently, a number of new elements such as direct income transfer, microfinance, and similar poverty alleviation programs have been added to the arsenal.

If one considers the first two elements of redistribution, the role of the Left will become very evident. The trade union and peasant movements and the consequent land reforms and institutions of collective bargaining were the direct contribution of the Left to modern Kerala. However, the history of the third element, public education and public healthcare, predates the emergence of the Left. From the latter half of the nineteenth century, the princely states in Travancore and Cochin took the initiative to promote public health and education. The Left extended this legacy of public provisioning of basic services, profoundly impacting the quality of life of ordinary people, the key indicators of which are summarised in Tables 4.1 and 4.2.

**Table 4.1 Comparison of social indicators of Kerala and India (1951, 2001, 2021)**

| Indicator | 1951 | 2001 | 2021 |
|---|---|---|---|
| 1. Literacy | | | |
| • Kerala | 40.7 | 90.9 | 96.2 |
| • India | 16.6 | 64.8 | 77.7[c] |
| 2. Infant Mortality Rate | | | |
| • Kerala | 153 | 11 | 7[b] |
| • India | 192* | 64.5 | 32[b] |
| 3. Maternal Mortality Rate (MMR) | | | |
| • Kerala | | 110 | 43[a] |
| • India | | 301 | 113[a] |
| 4. Life Expectancy | | | |
| • Kerala | 48.1 | 72.4 | 76.4 |
| • India | 41.9 | 62.9 | 70.9 |
| 5. Sex Ratio | | | |
| • Kerala | 1022 | 1058 | 1082 |
| • India | 941 | 933 | 945 |
| 6. Birth Rate | | | |
| • Kerala | 39.8 | 9.43 | 12.2 |
| • India | 39.9* | 21.5 | 16 |
| 7. Population Growth | | | |
| • Kerala | 22.8 | 9.4 | 5.2 |
| • India | 13.3 | 21.5 | 9.0 |
| 8. Per Capita Income (Rs .) Current Prices | | | |
| • Kerala | 259** | 28814 | 216749 |
| • India | 306** | 22261 | 145680 |

* Refers to 1941–1950.
** Numbers represent data in 1961.
a) Corresponds to figures in 2018. Source: Sample Registration System (SRS) report of Registrar General of India (RGI).
b) Corresponds to figures in 2018. Source: RBI States of India.
c) Data from NSO accessed from https://www.findeasy.in/indian-states-by-literacy-rate/.
Sources: Ramachandran (1997), Kerala State Planning Board (1987, 2018). Data for 2021 accessed from Census Population Projections.
Per capita incomes are in current prices.

## BASIC NEEDS ASSURED FOR EVERYONE

### *Education*

Let us first take up the issue of free and universal education. At the end of the colonial period, 40.7 per cent of Keralites were literate, 24.1 percentage points above the national average. By 2001 the difference had widened to 33.7 percentage points, and the state was nearly totally literate (Table 4.1, row 1). This was primarily the outcome of the spread of the school network and high social expenditure by the state government.

Today, the gross school enrolment in India is also above 100 at the elementary stage, but NFHS-5 in 2019–20 reveals that school attendance dropped as education levels increased. But the dropout rate was lowest in Kerala. Here the attendance in higher secondary school was 90.8 per cent for boys and 93.6 per cent for girls. At the lower end was Gujarat, with the school attendance at 45 per cent for boys and 29.2 per cent for girls in the higher secondary age group in the rural areas. The inequality in the access to secondary education, measured as the difference to access for those in the top and bottom quintiles of the distribution of household per capita income, is lowest in Kerala (Kingdom 2007).

In the School Education Quality Index (SEQUI) of NITI Aayog, Kerala, with a score of 77.6, was the highest-ranked in the country. SEQUI, which consists of a weighted average of 30 indicators – 14 indicators referring to learning, access, infrastructure, and equity outcomes and 16 related to governance process-aiding outcomes – is the most comprehensive assessment of the progress of education in different states.

### *Health*

The simplest measures of health standards are the Infant Mortality Rate (IMR) and the life expectancy numbers. The IMR tells us how many children survive for every thousand births till the age of one. The IMR for 1941–1950 was 153 for Kerala and 192 for India. By 2001, Kerala's IMR was 11 (India's 64.5). In 1951 the Maternal Mortality Rate (MMR) was 110 (Kerala) and 301 (India).

In 1951, the average Life Expectancy (LE) in the state was only 48 years and that in the country as a whole was even lower at 41.9 years. By 2001, the LE in Kerala was 72.4 years (India, 62.9 years). The life expectancy of females was higher than that of males. It is reflected in the sex ratio for the state. It is one of the few states with a positive sex ratio and increased from 1022 in 1951 to 1058 in 2001. In contrast, the national ratio declined from 941 to 933 during the same period.

*Shelter*

The housing conditions in Kerala are much better than rest of the country. Landlessness is lower and 80 per cent of the houses were *pucca* (the national average being 65). In 2011, 77 per cent of the houses in the state had drinking water in the premises, while in India, the ratio was 51 per cent. Ninety-five per cent of the houses were electrified as against the national average of 67 per cent. Ninety-five per cent of the houses had latrines, while in India, only 47 per cent of houses had such facilities. Ninety-three per cent of the houses in Kerala had more than one room, while the ratio in India was only 59 per cent (Kannan, Khan, 2016).

## DEMOGRAPHIC TRANSITION

By the end of the twentieth century, Kerala successfully completed the demographic transition from high mortality–high fertility regime to a low mortality-low fertility regime. The success in controlling epidemics through vaccination and other public health programs resulted in a decline in the death rate. However, the birth rate responds to the decline in death rate only with a time lag. We find that the birth rate in India and Kerala were similar at around 39 per cent in 1951 (Table 4.1, row 6). However, the death rate had started declining in Kerala. As a result, the first half of the twentieth century proved to be one of explosive growth in population, the decadal growth rate was 22.8 per cent during 1941–50 in the state while the national decadal growth rate was only 13.3 per cent (Table 4.1, row 7).

In the next phase, the birth rates also began to decline, and the decadal growth rate was 9.43 in 2001. The national average remained at a relatively high level of 21.54. Kerala has crossed the population hump.

## SUSTAINABLE DEVELOPMENT GOALS

The overall outcome of the above and related process has been the higher quality of life for average citizens, as reflected in numerous development indices given in Table 4.2. The most comprehensive of the indices is the SDG index to monitor the country's progress towards the UN General Assembly adopted 2030 agenda for sustainable development. It is a composite index of 100 indicators across 54 targets and 16 goals. Kerala was ranked 1 with a score of 75, the national average being 66. The Human Development Index is a composite of health and education indicators and per capita income prepared by UNDP. Kerala has consistently been at the front of the table.

## THE KERALA MODEL

From the above discussion, we may conclude two important points: One, even in the colonial period, Kerala was ahead of India in the key indicators of literacy, life expectancy, infant mortality, birth rate, and sex ratio. Two, surprisingly, the differential continued to widen during the last five decades of the twentieth century, that is, after independence. It is to focus on this aspect that we have chosen the year 2001 for comparison with 1951 in Table 4.1. It is only in the subsequent decades that the national averages catch up with Kerala.

**Table 4.2**

| Index | Organisation | Reference year | National average score | Kerala's score | Kerala's rank |
|---|---|---|---|---|---|
| 1. Sustainable Development Goals Index (SDG) | NITI Aayog | 2020 | 66 | 75.00 | 1 |
| 2. School Education Quality Index (SEQI) | NITI Aayog | 2021 | | 77.64 | 1 |
| 3. Health Index (HI) | NITI Aayog | 2015–16 | | 74.65 | 1 |
| 4. Human Development Index (HDI) | UNDP | 2018 | 0.647 | 0.79 | 1 |
| 5. Child Development Index (DCI) | India Child Well-being Report | 2019 | | 0.76 | 1 |

A surprising feature of this entire period was the relatively low level of economic development when compared to the rest of India. As we shall see in the next chapter, Kerala's economic development accelerated from the late 1980s, so in Table 4.1, Kerala's per capita income is already above the national average in 2001. The initial low economic development of Kerala is summarised in the per capita income, which in 1961 was Rs 259, while the national average per capita income of Rs 306.

This paradox was brought to the limelight in the debates generated by the seminal study by the Centre for Development Studies, directed by K.N. Raj in 1976. Though the study did not coin the phrase of 'Kerala Model,' the name stuck, Prof K.N. Raj tried to distance himself to the normative interpretations of the phrase (Raj, 1994). Over time, a vast body of literature has come up trying to explain its evolution, limitation, and sustainability.

If someone uses the phrase in a normative sense that everything in Kerala is fine and a model for emulation, it would be far removed from reality. E.M.S. Namboodiripad (1994), at one time, publicly aired his reservations with the phrase: 'let not the praise others shower on us deter us from clearly understanding the problems and challenges that the state is facing'.

Here we are using the phrase the 'Kerala Model' to denote a development paradigm that is quite different from the development paradigm of the western countries where high economic growth was the basis of trickledown redistribution. First growth, and then welfare, was their order of precedence. It was well after a century after the industrial revolution in the post-world war period that the concept of the welfare state became popular. This model has been sanctified by the celebrated economist Simon Kuznets, who posited that the income disparities would widen as the per capita income grows till it reaches the inflexion point of the curve.

The case of Kerala was a sharp contrast. Even at a low level of economic growth, the redistributive strategy contributed to a quality of life to its ordinary citizens more akin to the developed countries than their counterparts in other states of India or other underdeveloped countries. This outcome had the potential of a strong evocative appeal: one does not have to wait indefinitely for the economic growth to reach the summit before the minimum basic needs of the people are met. They can be achieved today, at the present level of economic growth, if only governments adopt an appropriate socio-political strategy for redistribution.

## BENEVOLENT ROYALTIES OR PEOPLE'S PRESSURE FROM BELOW?

Any narrative of the emergence of public education and health systems in the state should begin with missionaries and royalty. Starting from early nineteenth-century royal edicts, the setting up of institutions and announcement of regulations in the education and health sector by Travancore monarchs and the British advisers have been central to the growth of public education and health systems. Education and health care were also part of the evangelical mission of the Christian missionaries, and they set up the pioneering modern health and educational institutions, which came to be models for future interventions by the government as well as community organisations. (Ramankutty, 2000; Baru, 1999)

Without denying the importance of the pioneering efforts of royalty and missionaries in Travancore, it must also be understood that there were similar initiatives from the government and the missionaries in British India also. In fact, Michael Tharakan, whose studies have been seminal to understanding the social and economic factors behind education and development, has documented that every major royal edict in education has been preceded by similar proclamations in British India (Tharakan, 1986). Yet by the end of the colonial period, the density of hospitals, schools, doctors, teachers, and students in Travancore was far ahead of the rest of the country (Ramachandran, 1997).

While most of the pronouncements on education and health remained dead letters in British India, powerful social forces that successfully demanded their implementation were at play in Travancore. The role of demand from below in the public provisioning of health and education would be very evident if we compare their evolution in Travancore, a princely state, with Malabar, a region directly under British rule. Despite being part of the same linguistic region, the two administrative areas had divergent historical experiences in social sector development.

Even by the end of the nineteenth century, Malabar was lagging behind in social sector development. We find that the differences in the education and health indicators widened during the first half of the twentieth century between Malabar and Travancore-Kochi. Thus, for example, in 1901, the literacy rate in Malabar was 11.1 and Travancore 15.0 per cent. By 1951 the difference in the ratio had widened to 31.3 and 46.7 per cent, respectively (Ramachandran, 1997).

The divergent experience in social development between north and south Kerala has been attributed to the difference in the agrarian structures. Relatively weaker domination of landlordism in the south resulted in higher development capitalism and more acute social contradictions between the emerging middle and bourgeoise classes and traditional caste structures. The caste-class identity that we discussed in Table 3.1 was undermined because the new classes emerged from the ranks of middle castes and non-Hindu communities. We have already discussed how the situation gave rise to powerful social reform movements in the south.

The agricultural workers belonging to the lowest caste in south Travancore, under their charismatic leader Ayyankali conducted months-long agricultural strike demanding the right to study in public schools as far back as 1909 (Saradamani, 1980). The slogan for temple entry came decades after caste riots and violence related to school entry. The community organisations competed in setting up schools, and lower caste movements demanded and secured entry into public education. Such social intermediation was relatively weak in the north (Kabir and Krishnan, 1991).

Malabar region began to close the gap with the rest of Kerala after the unification and formation of Kerala. The first Communist government in 1957 initiated substantial investment in health and education facilities in the north. The popular demand for health and education gained momentum with the movement for land reforms and their implementation.

The anthropologist Joan Mencher in an article titled 'Lessons and Non-lessons of Kerala Model', has documented how a high level of awareness regarding entitlements in Kerala generated public protest if there was any lapse or denial of services in the Primary Health Care Centre in the Kerala village she was studying. This was a sharp contrast to the muted reactions from the public in the Tamil Nadu village that she took up for comparison (Mencher, 1980).

## THE WAGE ESCALATION AND THE LAND REFORMS

During the post-independence period, the dynamics were essentially the same: public demand for education and health services, now much more through the political process rather than socio-religious movements, forcing the successive governments in the state to step up public expenditure on health and education. The direct initiatives of local communities to set up educational and health institutions also became stronger.

The popular demand and agitation expanded beyond health and education sectors to other basic needs like village roads, drinking water, housing, and public distribution. The public distribution system in Kerala has its lineage in the local popular agitations in north Kerala against hoarding and demand for food coupons in the industrial belt of Alleppey during the War period. After prolonged agitation during the first half of the 60s, the central government was forced to sign an accord to introduce universal statutory rationing in this chronically food deficit state. The public distribution system contributed to improving the nutritional status of the poor.

It was in the post-independence period that the demands for higher wages by the trade unions and land reforms by the peasant movement came to be realised. As we noted in the last chapter, the formation of the first Communist ministry gave a fillip to the spread of trade unions, and wages began to rise. The wage rates gained momentum after the implementation of land reforms. An important institution that strengthened the upward movement of wages was the extension of minimum wages legislations and their periodic revisions. Today, it encompasses as many as 78 worker categories (Jose, 2021). Another factor that helped the rapid rise in the wage rates has been the external migration of construction workers and the consequent increase in their wages. This extraneous factor had a cascading impact on other relative wages based on popular moral notions of relative wages in different sectors and their parity (Krishnan, 1991).

By the 1980s, the wages for field labourers in the state were nearly double the national average. However, its impact on the earnings of the workers has been dampened by a decline in the days of employment. Underemployment in the state is the highest in the country, and on average, casual workers days of employment have shrunk to 3 to 4 days in a week. The crisis was averted by an increase in the social wage through various social provisioning by the state. In some of the traditional industries, the state government supplements the daily income of the workers by as much as 30 per cent through a scheme introduced by the Left government in 2007 called the Income Support Scheme. During the last two decades, the increase in wages has tended to plateau off after the in-migration of casual workers from other states who are attracted to Kerala because of the higher wages.

The impact of land reforms has been greatest in northern Kerala, where the tenancy was widely prevalent. In 1951 the rentier landlords, who constituted 4 per cent of the agrarian population, controlled more than 70 per cent of the land in Malabar. The landless tenants constituted 39 per cent of the agricultural workforce. The land-owning cultivators were only 13 per cent. Landless agricultural workers accounted for another 44 per cent of the agricultural workforce. This agrarian structure underwent a dramatic change with the land reforms. The land renting landlords exited from the scene. Since tenancy was abolished, the category of landless cultivators also disappeared. The number of land-owning cultivators increased from 13 per cent to around 40 per cent. In Kerala as a whole, 28 lakh tenants became landowners. The proportion of the agricultural workers swelled to around 60 per cent. As explained already, the implementation of land ceiling provisions of the Land Reform Act was not successful, and as a result, the agricultural worker households could gain only their hutment land. Their unionisation rapidly spread, and wages improved.

The land reforms also undermined to an extent the economic base of upper-caste domination in Kerala. The landlords and superior tenants were generally from upper castes, and therefore land reforms implied a major shift of land ownership to lower castes. The worst forms of caste discrimination, such as pollution norms, had disappeared from public life by then, and the land reforms strengthened the upward social mobility of lower castes.

## THE SECOND-GENERATION CHALLENGES AND CRISIS OF PUBLIC SYSTEMS

Success breeds its own challenges. An increase in life expectancy and changes in lifestyle resulted in a shift in morbidity patterns towards geriatric problems and lifestyle diseases such as diabetes, hypertension, heart ailments, cancer, and so on that could not be fully addressed by the existing public health system. With single child families becoming the norm, parents wanted better facilities in the schools and quality education. Free and universal schooling through the public education system (government schools and private aided schools) slipped behind the popular aspiration levels as per capita incomes improved.

A major upgradation of education and health facilities was required. However, with the growing fiscal crisis of the state, which we shall discuss in detail in the next chapter, the required public investment was not forthcoming. Professor K.K. George (1993) first drew attention to this phenomenon with 'The Limits to Kerala Model'. He showed that the share of education and health sectors in the overall government expenditure, as well as the plan expenditure, declined between 1974–75 to 1984–85. The capacity of the state government to undertake new schemes (plan) but also service the past schemes (non-plan) was eroded by the financial squeeze, impacting the quality of services. The per capita expenditure on health and education declined below some of the other states. This tightening of budget constraints was taking place at a time when the second-generation challenges in the social sectors were becoming prominent.

When the government cut back on investments in education and health, the private sector stepped in to meet the demand-supply gap. The middle class increasingly began to shift towards unaided private schools whose enrolments increased from 1.5 lakhs students in 1991 to 3.6 lakhs by the mid-2000s and peaked at 4.1 lakhs in 2016–17 (Vimalan, 2019). The percentage of persons using government facilities declined to 34 per cent in the 71st round of the NSSO (2015). As a consequence, private health costs escalated, and the poor were getting marginalised (Sadanandan, 2001; Ekbal, 2006, 2019). This process also began to affect the health outcomes. The epidemic breakouts such as dengue fever and chikungunya became common. The levels of anaemia among children went up. Disconcertingly, the IMR increased to 15 in 2006 (Thresia, 2013).

What was the solution? Privatisation was the neoliberal answer. The data confirm the global trends of market-driven education reform towards privatisation (Zajda, 2006; Kumar and George, 2009). But it would have delivered a body blow to the inclusive development paradigm and severely undermined the progressive and secular civic culture of Kerala. Universal education, where all children irrespective of caste, religion, or wealth shared a common experience in their formative years, was an important factor in its making. Participation rather than privatisation was proposed as the alternative.

## Chapter 5

# The Evolution of the Economy: Stagnation, Growth, and its Challenges

Redistribution rather than growth was the defining feature of the Kerala economy. Relatively high quality of life for the average citizen at a relatively low per capita income came to be acclaimed as the Kerala model. However, there was also a strong line of thinking that there would be a trade-off between equity and growth. Recall the Kuznets curve that we referred to in the last chapter? Was the state's economic stagnation an outcome of the focus on distribution from the early stages of modern economic growth?

The growth scenario changed even while the debate on growth and equity gathered momentum. Kerala was transformed from a low per capita income-consumption-saving-investment and consequently slow-growing backward economy to a high per capita income-consumption-saving and fast-growing economy. What was the catalyst?

What is the worry after such a happy outcome? It is crucial we understand the failure of the new phase of economic growth to address the second-generation challenges of Kerala's development and problems of the educated unemployed.

In response to these critical questions, we are undertaking a broad sweep of the state's economic growth in the post-independence period in the present chapter.

## THE TWO PHASES: SLOTH (1961 TO 1987) AND GROWTH (1988 TO 2018)

A paradox of the Kerala economy was the contrast between

**Table 5.1 Annual Growth Performance of Kerala (1960-61 to 2018-19)**

| | 1961-1987 | 1988-2018 | 1988-1996 | 1961-2018 |
|---|---|---|---|---|
| GDP Growth | 2.93 | 6.71 | 6.72 | 4.83 |
| Per-capita Income Growth | 0.99 | 6.00 | 5.71 | 3.53 |
| Agriculture GDP Growth | 1.25 | 1.30 | 5.35 | 1.03 |
| Industry GDP Growth | 4.70 | 7.20 | 8.54 | 5.89 |
| Service GDP Growth | 4.43 | 7.89 | 6.90 | 6.28 |

Source: Calculated from national income data, EPWRF.

the sectoral distribution of its employment and income. The percentage of employed in non-agriculture sectors in 1961 was 44 per cent of Kerala's workforce, giving a mistaken impression of a relatively advanced economy. The somewhat higher proportion of the workforce in the secondary and tertiary sector compared to the national average of around 30 per cent was more a reflection of the backward nature and low productivity of its non-agricultural sectors. The contribution of the non-agricultural sector in the total output was only 45 per cent. In fact, the relative sectoral product per worker in the industry at 0.72 was lower than that of agriculture at 0.99 (Centre for Development Studies, 1975, p. 81). Given the relatively low labour force absorption by the commercial crops that dominated agriculture, the surplus population was accommodated mainly in the low productivity handicraft industries and traditional service sectors. The large population dependent upon traditional handicraft industries was a major impediment to their modernisation. As a result, the per capita income of Kerala was lower than the national average.

The trend in economic growth during the period 1961–2018 is summarised in Table 5.1. In the first four decades of independence, until the end of the 1980s, the economy grew at a slow rate of 2.9 per cent. From the mid-1960s to the mid-1970s, the growth rate picked up some momentum, but it was more than undone by the severe stagnation in the subsequent period. The national economy grew during this period at 3.92 per cent per annum. In other words, Kerala's economic performance was worse than India's.

It was the lack of adequate investment that constrained the growth. The initial decade of independence was a washout. In the industrial sector, the European West Coast Trading Companies and Tamil Chettiar capital, which were imparting some level of dynamism into the industrial sector of Travancore-Cochin in the pre-independence period, began to withdraw from the region. The Malayali entrepreneurs were 'still at the stage of capitalist development when projects which promise easy as well as pick money, and even speculative enterprises, seem to have considerable appeal to those who have a reasonable amount of capital' (Raj, 1960). There was not a single industry that came up in Kerala during this period. Because of the numerous administrative reorganisations in the first decade of independence and political instability, no substantial public investment took place. By the time the state was formed, the second five-year plan was already formulated. There was some dynamism in the economy in the latter half of the 1960s, but as we have noted, it was short-lived as the national economy by then had fallen into a major crisis (Isaac and Tharakan, 1986).

There was a considerable investment for the expansion of commercial agriculture. However, the landlord agrarian structure in Malabar was a significant impediment to investment (Shea, 1959; Varghese, 1970). The shift in cropping pattern to commercial crops, which required substantial investment, accelerated after the land reforms. However, the output from the long gestation crops would get reflected in the agricultural income only after a few years. This also aggravated the apparent stagnation in agriculture (Narayana, 1990).

While policymakers and scholars were engrossed in trying to understand the puzzling stagnation of the regional economy, the trend was changing. But it took nearly two decades before the turnaround was noticed (Kannan, 2005; Chakravarthy, 2005). As can be seen from Table 5.1, the average annual growth rate accelerates 2.93 per cent during 1961–1987 to 6.71 per cent in the period 1988–2018.

The agriculture growth does not show any overall improvement in performance. The expansion of commercial crops began to get reflected in agricultural output, and the average growth of agriculture increased from 1.25 per cent during the first phase to 5.35 per cent during the decade of 1988–1998. Then the agricultural sector collapsed after a synchronized steep fall in all the commercial corps prices. The liberalisation of imports of agricultural products and the ASEAN Free Trade Agreement dealt a devastating blow to the prospects of agriculture. The Commodity Boards, which are primarily responsible for the commercial crops, turned a Nelson's eye to the crisis, nay, they themselves were largely disembowelled by the central government. The result was that the overall agricultural growth went negative at -1.23 per cent.

However, the industrial and service sectors kept up the momentum growing at 7.2 per cent and 7.89 per cent. Given the rapid decline of the household industries and the slow expansion of the large-scale factory sector, the Micro Small Medium Enterprises (MSME) sector displayed vigorous growth. Within the service sectors, the administrative services and consumption-related services were more buoyant.

The overall outcome of the above trends was that the per capita income growth, aided by the slow growth of the population, accelerated from 0.99 per cent per annum during the first phase to 6 per cent per annum during the second phase. In 1960–61 it was Rs 259 as against the national average of Rs 306, which is 15 per cent lower. By 1987–88 it was 22 per cent lower. Since then, the trend has reversed, and it rose above the national average by 1993–94. In 2017–18 the ratio of per capita income of the state to the national average was 56 per cent above the national average (Kerala State Planning Board, 1988, 1990, 2020). Kerala's national ranking of states by per capita income improved from 12$^{th}$ in 1987 to 5$^{th}$ in 2018 among the big states.

## THE IMPACT OF GROWTH ON MACRO ECONOMIC VARIABLES

The acceleration of growth significantly impacted different macro-economic variables like consumption, saving, investment, terms of trade, and regional trade balance.

### *Consumption*

The low level of consumption in the state was a matter of serious debate during the first phase. The very low level of food consumption contrasted with Kerala's health attainments that Professor P.G.K. Panicker was prompted to prepare a food balance sheet for Kerala. He proved that if the home-grown products of homestead gardens, which were omitted in the nutritional survey, are also considered, the consumption would become more respectable, though still lower than the national standards (Centre for Development Studies, 1975 pp. 157–182).

In 1970–71, the per capita consumption of Rs 456 was marginally below the national average and Kerala was adjudged 8th in the national ranking. In the second phase, the per capita consumption in the state was around 25 per cent higher than the national average; Kerala's rank moved to one among the first three. There were also significant changes in the composition of consumption from cheap carbohydrate substitutes like tubers to costlier cereals and animal protein. The share of non-food items expanded, and within the non-food basket, consumer durables rose to prominence. In national ranking, Kerala's position in per capita consumption improved to first or second (Isaac, 1992)

### *Saving*

There are no reliable estimates of regional savings or savings rates. But there are two sources of information that indicate an increase in the financial and physical savings of the state during the second phase. First is the average value of assets of rural households revealed by All India Rural Debt and Investment Surveys. Till the 1980s, the average value of assets of Kerala households was only near the average, and the rank position was constant at 8. Then it improved dramatically to second, next only to Punjab (Ibid.).

The next evidence is related to the trend in per capita deposits of the commercial banks which was lower by more than 20 per cent of the national average till the mid-1970s. Thereafter it rose to more than 20 per cent above the national average (Ibid.).

*Investment*

The investment in Kerala has also picked up. But it, by and large, bypassed the agricultural and industrial sectors and has been chiefly in construction, trade, finance, and other service sectors. Therefore, industrial growth has tended to lag behind other sectors, adversely affecting employment generation. The bank credit deposit ratio remained below the national average, indicating a significant outflow of financial savings.

*Terms of Trade*

Since colonial times, Kerala's regional economy has been closely integrated with the national and world economy. It exports around 60–65 per cent of its domestic production and imports around 70–75 per cent of its consumption and intermediate products from outside. A significant factor advantageous to Kerala has been the favourable relative price of imports to exports, i.e., the terms of trade. However, as we have noted in chapter 1, with the implementation of liberalisation reforms, the terms of trade have become unfavourable. A relatively better economic performance has been achieved despite this handicap (Isaac et al., 1992).

*Regional Trade Balance*

During most of the first phase, Kerala was a regional economy with a positive trade balance, which was, in fact, a reflection of the backwardness of its economy. However, from the mid-1970s, the trade balance has become negative, and the gap has been widening (Isaac et al., 1992). This external dependence dampened the multiplier impact of remittances.

In short, the Kerala economy has undergone a profound transformation from a slow-growing low per capita income economy to a fast-growing high per capita income economy. Attendant to this transformation has been an increase in consumption, savings, and investment. However, it is also evident that Kerala was failing to utilise the new opportunity to overcome its backwardness in the material production sectors. The regional trade deficit and terms of trade worsened.

## MIGRATION, REMITTANCE IN-FLOW, AND CONSEQUENCES

What has catalysed the above-described profound transformation of the Kerala economy? The prime mover was the rapid expansion of migration to Gulf countries resulting in an inflow of remittances. Starting from the 1930s, inter-regional migration of educated youth from Kerala to urban centres of India became a common phenomenon. Kerala was also a participant in the post-independence period migration of skilled and professional workers to Western countries. The decisive break came with opening job opportunities in the Gulf countries after the oil boom in the mid-1970s. The average annual net migration to Gulf countries at the end of the 1970s was estimated to be around 70,000. By the end of the 1980s, it had increased to 500,000. The stock of migrants from Kerala in the Gulf countries increased to approximately 1.4 million at the end of the 1990s (Kannan and Hari, 2020; Zachariah and Rajan, 2016).

There have been many exercises to estimate the inflow of remittances to Kerala (Gulati and Modi, 1983; Nayyar, 1989; Kannan and Hari, 2020; Rajan and Zachariah, 2020). The picture that emerges is that the remittance inflow as a ratio of NSDP was negligible in 1970–71. It began to surge upwards from 2.06 per cent in 1975–76 to 12.64 per cent in 1986–87 and further to 24.5 per cent in 1996–97. Since then, it has tended to plateau off. It must be cautioned that these estimates do not include the remittances through the *hawala* route, which were considerable before 1991, anything between 20 to 50 per cent of the official remittance.

There is a popular line of thinking that the remittances were like manna from the heavens, saving the Kerala economy. On the other hand, we would argue that out-migration and inflow of remittances were an outcome of considerable investment in human resources made in the state. The study by the Centre for Development Studies in 1975, before the gulf migration boom, had concluded that 'it appears likely that investment in education in Kerala has promoted the mobility of its population in search of employment elsewhere and, by helping it to acquire other skills, enabled it to secure such employment in more rapidly developing areas in the country. Such skill formation could prove to be a major factor in the next stage of development in Kerala.' (Centre for Development Studies, 1975 p. 152) There is also no need to deny the historical link of Kerala with Gulf countries; serving as an inter-port between the Far East and the Middle East from ancient times. This factor provided Kerala with a head start.

From the 2000s, the net-out migration began to decline and has become negative in recent years. The remittance inflow has also significantly decelerated, raising the prospects of a reverse multiplier impact, creating very serious social and political repercussions. Such a prospect is like a sword of Damocles hanging above the regional economy. This is yet another reason for the sense of urgency adopting a strategy of development that would also focus on revamping the economic base to accelerate growth and generate employment for the educated workforce, which we shall be discussing in Chapter 9.

## THE CHALLENGE OF EDUCATED UNEMPLOYMENT

The acceleration of growth has not been sufficiently effective to make a dent in the chronically high unemployment situation in the state. Table 5.2 reveals certain significant features of this unemployment situation. One, the unemployment rate in Kerala has increased from 3.69 per cent in 1973–74 to peak at 18.5 per cent in 2004–05 and then tended to decline and plateau off. Two, the unemployment rate in the state has been higher than the national average. The unemployment rate in the country also has tended to increase but at much a slower rate.

Unemployment in Kerala was nearly three times higher than the national average in 1973–74. The ratio increased to nearly six times by 2004–05. Thereafter the difference has continuously declined. Currently, it is only double the national average. Nevertheless, unemployment, particularly of the educated sectors, remains the most important challenge to the policymakers in the state.

Unemployment among women, interestingly, was below men till the early 1980s. Then, the situation reversed, and the female unemployment rate was more than double that of the male unemployment rate. The ratio steadily increased five-fold in 2009–10. Thereafter it has declined to 3.4 times in 2018–19.

Because of high unemployment, the labour force participation of females is very much lower than the male labour force participation. Mainly because of this, the labour force participation rate in Kerala has been lower than the national average.

One important reason for the relatively high open (as opposed to disguised) unemployment in Kerala is because of the wide prevalence of wage labour relations. The spread of education makes it difficult to disguise unemployment. Among the educated, the preference for formal sector employment is strong, and they tend to shift away from traditional occupations. Their preferred reserve status and reserve emolument level tend to rise. They

**Table-5.2 Unemployment Rate in Kerala and All India (per cent) Usual Status 1973–74/2018–19**

| | Male | | Female | | Total | |
|---|---|---|---|---|---|---|
| | Kerala | All India | Kerala | All India | Kerala | All India |
| 1973–74 | 4.9 | 1.9 | 2.5 | 0.7 | 3.7 | 1.3 |
| 1983–84 | 5.0 | 2.0 | 3.6 | 0.6 | 4.3 | 1.3 |
| 1993–94 | 8.8 | 2.7 | 19.1 | 3.5 | 12.1 | 2.9 |
| 1999–00 | 8.5 | 3.1 | 23.0 | 3.4 | 13.3 | 3.1 |
| 2004–05 | 8.2 | 2.7 | 36.8 | 4.4 | 18.5 | 3.1 |
| 2009–10 | 4.7 | 2.2 | 24.5 | 3.7 | 11.2 | 2.5 |
| 2011–12 | 4.5 | 2.4 | 21.2 | 3.5 | 9.9 | 2.6 |
| 2017–18 | 9.2 | 6.5 | 33.4 | 7.3 | 16.6 | 6.6 |
| 2018–19 | 7.3 | 6.4 | 25.0 | 6.7 | 13.3 | 6.4 |

Notes: Employment figures are the sum of principal status and subsidiary status.

Source: From 1983–84 to 2011–12, various rounds Employment and Unemployment Survey NSSO; 2017–18 and 2019–20 from Periodic Labour Force Survey (PLFS) NSSO.

would consider themselves unemployed till they attain their preferred reserve status.

The limited job opportunities for the preferred status jobs tend to prolong the waiting period of educated job seekers and thereby increase their stock. Available evidence points to a four-fold increase in the waiting period between 1976 and 1989 (Mukherjee and Isaac, 1994). As a survival strategy, many among the educated unemployed are forced to seek employment in the informal sectors, which are low paying and do not guarantee any security of tenure but are nearer to their perceived reserve job status. This to an extent mitigates against the severity of deprivation of prolonged unemployment.

Given the socio-economic level and gender, a higher educational qualification raises the probability of getting employment, even if non-commensurate with the qualification. It would also, to an extent, help the unemployed to overcome socio-economic handicaps. Consequently, the pursuit of higher qualifications has become an important adjustment mechanism during the waiting period. We have yet another paradoxical situation: demand for education continues to rise despite growing unemployment among the educated.

Finally, the incidence of unemployment and the waiting period is much higher among educated females even though their job expectations are relatively lower than males. An important outcome of a prolonged waiting period is the discouraged dropout of females from the labour force itself, resulting in a much lower participation rate of women.

Along with the second-generation challenges in the social sectors, the major challenge that the state must address is the unacceptable level of unemployment. It is appropriate at this juncture that we turn attention to the fiscal capacity of the state government to shoulder these challenges.

## FISCAL CRISIS OF THE STATE GOVERNMENT

The inflow of remittances and rapid improvement in consumption expanded the tax base of the government. However, in Table 5.3, we find that the tax-GSDP (Gross State Domestic Product) ratio, after improving from 5.45 per cent during the 1960s to 7 per cent in the 1970s, has not kept pace with the expansion of GSDP in the subsequent decades. It sharply declined to 5.51 per cent in the 1980s and has tended to slowly rise and is still below the 1970s record. But the own tax-GSDP ratio of Kerala was higher than all states average ratio. The tax buoyancy was higher than other states.

At the same time, the revenue receipts to GSDP ratio of Kerala is seen to be lower than the national average. This is because of the declining central transfers to the state government. It has declined from 2.15 per cent in 1980–89 to 1.71 per cent during 2000–09. Though it has increased to 1.93 per cent in the next decade, it is much lower than the overall central transfers to all states GSDP of 3.28 (Table 5.3, row 2).

**Table 5.3 Comparative Statement of Selected Fiscal Ratios of Kerala and All States Average to GSDP**

| Item | Kerala/ All States | 1961-1969 | 1970-1979 | 1980-1989 | 1990-1999 | 2000-2009 | 2010-2018 |
|---|---|---|---|---|---|---|---|
| 1. Share of own tax revenue to GSDP | Kerala | 5.45 | 7.00 | 5.51 | 6.12 | 6.50 | 6.91 |
| | All states | NA | 5.86 | 5.45 | 5.32 | 5.9 | 6.3 |
| 2. Share of central transfers to GSDP | Kerala | 1.80 | 2.84 | 2.15 | 1.95 | 1.71 | 1.93 |
| | All states | NA | 2.75 | 2.72 | 2.56 | 2.69 | 3.28 |
| 3. Revenue expenditure to GSDP | Kerala | 12.92 | 15.15 | 10.68 | 11.67 | 12.23 | 13.40 |
| | All states | NA | 12.62 | 12.27 | 12.84 | 13.18 | 13.99 |
| 4. Capital expenditure to GSDP | Kerala | 1.97 | 2.35 | 2.08 | 1.55 | 0.95 | 1.36 |
| | All states | NA | 2.48 | 3.49 | 2.27 | 2.47 | 2.75 |
| 5. Total expenditure to GSDP | Kerala | 14.89 | 17.50 | 12.76 | 13.23 | 13.18 | 14.76 |
| | All states | NA | 15.10 | 15.75 | 15.11 | 15.65 | 16.74 |
| 6. Social expenditure to GSDP | Kerala | 7.35 | 8.04 | 5.60 | 4.76 | 4.15 | 4.90 |
| | All states | NA | 5.08 | 5.23 | 4.89 | 4.97 | 5.64 |
| 7. Education expenditure to GSDP | Kerala | 4.20 | 5.38 | 3.26 | 2.91 | 2.42 | 2.58 |
| | All states | NA | 2.65 | 2.61 | 2.63 | 2.46 | 2.57 |
| 8. Health expenditure to GSDP | Kerala | 1.26 | 1.53 | 1.13 | 0.74 | 0.60 | 0.76 |
| | All states | NA | 1.13 | 1.13 | 0.72 | 0.58 | 0.64 |
| 9. Revenue deficit to GSDP | Kerala | -0.06 | -0.11 | -0.46 | -1.62 | -2.43 | -2.18 |
| | All states | NA | -1.06 | -0.08 | -1.23 | -1.07 | -0.05 |
| 10. Fiscal deficit to GSDP | Kerala | 1.91 | 2.24 | -2.54 | -3.18 | -3.38 | -3.54 |
| | All states | NA | 1.42 | -3.06 | -3.17 | -3.29 | -2.49 |

Note: In the absence of GSDP data, NSDP data is used from 1960–61 to 1979–80. All states average for 1970 to 1979 shows the average of 1972–79.
Source: Calculated from a database of EPWRF and Budget in brief, Kerala (1961–72).

Given the above pattern of revenue receipts of Kerala and all states, it is not surprising that the revenue expenditure to GSDP of the state has always been lower than the all-states average. However, the difference between Kerala and the all-states average has tended to come down over time from 1.59 percentage points during the 1980s to 0.59 during the latest decade (Table 5.3, row 3). The increase in revenue expenditure has been facilitated by a squeeze on capital expenditure which declined from 2.09 per cent during the 1980s to 0.95 per cent during the 2000s. It can be seen from Table 5.3 (row 4) that the capital expenditure ratio to GSDP of all states average has been higher than that of Kerala throughout. The overall expenditure of the Kerala state government has tended to increase from 12.76 per cent during the 1980s to 14.76 during the latest decade. They have always been below the all-states average.

These figures are a very surprising finding because, being an activist state, we would have expected the overall expenditure of the Kerala government would be relatively higher than other states. This points to a fiscal constraint within which the Kerala government is operating. Table 5.3 (rows 7,8) also shows that during the 1960s and 1970s, Kerala was spending more on education and healthcare than other states. However, by the turn of the century, the other states caught up with Kerala. This is evident in the overall social expenditure to GSDP ratio, which during the 1980s was 5.6 per cent in Kerala and 5.23 per cent in all states on average. During the present decade, the ratios are 4.9 per cent and 5.64 per cent, respectively.

The widening of revenue receipts and revenue expenditure of the state government resulted in a worsening of the revenue deficit to GSDP ratio from -0.46 during the 1980s to -2.43 during the 2000s. In the next decade, before the COVID-19 pandemic, it has tended to decline to -2.18. Most of the other states were still in a revenue surplus during the 1980s. During the 1990s, the combined revenue deficit to GSDP was -1.23 and steadily declined thereafter, most of them becoming revenue surplus once again (Table 5.3, row 9).

The decadal averages revealed that the fiscal deficit of Kerala has been worsening from -2.54 during the 1980s to -3.54 during 2010–18. All states average fiscal deficit, which had been rising to 3.29 per cent during the 2000s, sharply declined to 2.49 during 2010–18 (Table 5.3, row 10). In short, fiscal consolidation in Kerala has been tardy. And more importantly, the state has been forced to deploy a large share of its borrowed funds for social expenditure, thereby adversely affecting capital expenditure. Even after this diversion, the fund allocation for social sectors like health and education was inadequate to meet the burgeoning needs. This was 'the Limits to Kerala Model of Development' that Professor K.K. George was speaking about, which we referred to in the previous chapter.

Chapter 6

# Response to the Crisis: Democratic Decentralization and People's Plan

'The Left must have a program to bake more bread before redistributing it. You have proved to be good at distribution. But you have no program for production'. This was a common criticism by many liberals in the background of acute stagnation of the Kerala economy from the late 1970s. EMS was a leader who fully understood the nature of the development challenge that Kerala was facing: 'Let not the praise that scholars shower on Kerala for its achievements divert attention from the intense economic crisis that we face. We are behind other states of India in respect of economic growth, and a solution to this crisis brooks no delay. We can ignore our backwardness in respect of employment and production only at our own peril' (Namboodiripad, 1994).

EMS initiated a development dialogue in which all the scholars on Kerala and many of the leading socio-political activists were brought together periodically. Four such conclaves have been organised so far. The first of these, the International Congress on Kerala Studies in 1994, chaired by EMS, brought together around 1600 people (nearly 700 being academic scholars from more than two dozen disciplines) from nearly two dozen countries and all the major states in India. Spread over three days in 60 technical sessions and six symposia, the participants presented and discussed over 600 papers. Altogether 170 hours of discussion took place in 17 parallel venues of the Congress. The abstracts of the papers presented at the Congress were compiled in five volumes and distributed to the participants (Isaac and Tharakan, 1995).

An important line of thinking at the Congress was that

democratic decentralisation would be a suitable response to the problems related to petty production, including agriculture and improvement in the quality of services. The 73rd and 74th constitutional amendments made the third tier of local governments a formal part of the constitutional structure. This provided an opportunity to realise this important unfinished agenda of the 1957 government. Democratic decentralisation was to be the main agenda of the Left government that came to power in 1996.

## THE POLITICAL STRATEGY BEHIND THE PEOPLE'S PLAN CAMPAIGN

The decision of the new LDF government in 1996 to earmark 35–40 per cent of the outlay of the state's Ninth Five Year Plan as untied funds to the local governments startled everyone. It was evident that the normal preconditions for such a radical financial devolution like redeployment of staff, formulation of procedures and rules, training of personnel and other administrative reforms would take a fairly long period to be satisfied. 'Common sense' called for restraint and a gradualist approach. This had been the excuse always held out to postpone the devolution. No one can ever learn to swim without jumping into the water. It was indeed a big bang launch.[1]

It was decided to launch a People's Planning Campaign (PPC) to rally behind the elected local bodies, the officials, the experts, and the masses of people so that the handicaps could be overcome, and local plans are prepared from below keeping the schedule for the Ninth Plan. The Campaign was also expected to bring about certain basic attitudinal changes towards the development process among all the stakeholders involved — the elected representatives, officials, experts, and the people at large. A radical transformation

[1] The discussion of PPC in this chapter is essentially based on our analysis in Isaac and Franke (2021)

of the development culture of the state was a necessary prerequisite for successful participatory decentralisation.

There is, however, a crucial question: How does one ensure that the new values and spirit generated do not die away with the tide of the movement but are sustained? In the long run, the sustainability of the new development culture depends upon the success in institutionalising it in the legal system, new developmental institutions, and traditions. Changes in laws and statutes or the legalisation of new institutions would not occur automatically. There must be sustained pressure from below, i. e., of the masses, mobilised in the movement for decentralisation, to secure the necessary structural changes.

In short, devolution was not to be a mere administrative reform from above but also a mass movement from below. The lessons of past failed attempts at decentralisation were well learnt. As in the case of land reforms, mobilisation of people cutting across the political divide was necessary for generating the political will to carry out the fundamental break in the governance system. The motive behind the advance announcement of this unparalleled scale of fiscal devolution was to kick start the movement.

Before the local governments could claim their fiscal entitlement, they would have to draw up a plan for spending the money allotted. A detailed six-stage planning procedure was laid down. The objective of the procedures was threefold: One, to encourage maximum participation of people in the decision-making process and ensure that nobody was excluded. Two, to promote transparency, for which the procedures emphasised written documentation, which was not difficult in a literate society like Kerala. Three, to ensure an informed, scientific, and deliberative decision-making process.

In a sense, the Left government was setting in motion a mass mobilisation process which would also foreclose its options and hesitations. It was like crossing the bridge and then breaking the bridge. There was no option to retreat but only to march forward.

Many have considered it a paradox that the Communists who are committed to democratic centralisation have been the biggest practitioners of democratic decentralisation as exhibited by the measures adopted by Left governments, not only in Kerala but also in West Bengal and Tripura. The explanation is simple, democratic centralisation is the organisational principle of the party but not of society. E.M.S. Namboodiripad (1978), in his note of dissent to the Ashok Mehta Committee Report on Panchayati Raj Institutions, stated, 'Defence of Parliamentary democracy at Central and State level (where it exists but is very often threatened by the authoritarian forces) and its extension to the district and lower levels as envisaged in the four-pillar democracy is, therefore, of extreme importance in the advance of Indian society . . . it helps the working people in their day-to-day struggles against their oppressors and exploiters'.

Our emphasis on the political strategy of the Left in no way diminishes the role played by civil society organisations in the decentralisation process. Kerala could embark upon the road to comprehensive local level planning because the ground was already prepared through numerous local level development experiments during the preceding decade. Most important among these organisations was the people's science movement (Kerala Sasthara Sahithya Parishath or KSSP), whose sweep and influence would be comparable to the library movement that successfully promoted literacy and political involvement earlier in the twentieth century. Its most important contributions have been in the education and health sectors and local level planning (Zacharia and Moorthy, 1994). From the total literacy movement to people's resource mapping and thence to village level planning was the path it traversed. COSTFORD, an organisation set up by architect Laurie Baker, erstwhile Chief Minister C. Achutha Menon and the academic K.N. Raj, was yet another organisation involved in alternative building technology and planning. There were church-related diocesan development organisations, semi-governmental organisations and even individuals who were experimenting with alternative paradigms. The People's Plan Campaign freely drew from this vast body of experience for techniques of planning and models of local development.

The neoliberal approach to 'decentralisation' visualises a substitution of the state by a set of NGOs in the implementation of local projects, especially social sector projects, the funds for which, whether drawn from the state budget or from foreign donors, are expended through these NGOs, who need not be accountable to the people (Patnaik 2004). The civil society actors will continue to play an important role in the development process in Kerala. But their interventions must be within the framework of the local plan. The local governments are the central fulcrum of the decentralisation process.

From the outset, the PPC demarcated itself from neoliberal decentralisation programs that were being advocated by international agencies like the World Bank as part of their structural adjustment programs. It drew inspiration from the Grama Swaraj of the national movement. Local planning and not the 'free market' was the central fulcrum around which the decentralisation in Kerala unfolded. Devolution can be a strategic response of the 'affirmative democratic state' to the neoliberal onslaught (Fung and Wright, 2003).

The Kerala PPC was thus a part of a larger political vision as in the case of the Participatory Budgeting (PB) promoted by the Left parties and social movements during the 'Pink Tide' (Spronk, 2008; Baiocchi, 1999; Ganuza and Baiocchi, 2012) in Latin America. As Prabhat Patnaik wrote of the PPC (2004),

> It provides a legacy for the construction of a better society. Any socialist society must build on the institutions bequeathed to it by the pre-existing society. Indeed, a part of the reason for the excessive centralisation, and the accompanying authoritarianism, that prevailed in the earlier socialist societies

lay in the absence of any representative democratic institutions in these societies prior to the emergence of socialism on which the latter could build its foundations. In that sense, the decentralisation experiment, by empowering elected bodies, puts life into a whole range of institutions based on which a future society can be built.

However, the above claim raises an important question: If the PPC was indeed a political project of the Left in Kerala, how come the non-Left governments in Kerala continued the project? How do the local governments under the non-Left political formations perform within the PPC framework?

This was precisely the challenge: how to design a programme platform that could accommodate a diversity of views and multiple party formations? What democratic decentralisation achieves is the creation of a democratic space at the local level for popular mobilisation and democratisation. Who would occupy this space and how they would utilise it is a matter of political contestation. The outcome would be open.

## LOCAL LEVEL PLANNING AND IMPLEMENTATION PROCESS

From the preceding discussion, we can see that the process of planning becomes as important as the final product, the local plans. The guidelines of the Planning Commission or different committees on decentralised planning were of little use in this respect. This was because they did not envisage the participation of people or even local governments in the local planning process. Further, their reference point was either the district or the block. Kerala was attempting a bottom-up planning process from grama panchayats to the higher tiers. A simple but effective six-phase planning procedure was drawn up.

The local development problems were identified by the people of every locality in their grama sabhas and ward sabhas. It was estimated that nearly two million persons participated in these first rounds of grama sabhas, i.e., at least around one-fourth of the households in Kerala were represented in the grama sabhas.

In the next step, the needs listed below were prioritised by delegates of the gram sabhas in development seminars. Before the development seminars, an objective assessment of the resource potential and development problems in each sector was prepared — secondary data were collected from government offices, geographical studies undertaken through transect walks, local history written, ongoing schemes reviewed, and grama sabha reports consolidated. These comprehensive Area Development Reports of 75–100 pages were the basic documents for the discussion at the Development Seminars. It was estimated that more than 3 lakh delegates attended these seminars.

The seminars constituted a task force for each of the development sectors to prepare the prioritised proposals for projects. Nearly one lakh persons served in these task forces. A simple and transparent format was suggested to be uniformly followed in the preparation of the projects.

At the end of the third phase, every grama panchayat and municipality had a shelf of projects corresponding to the development problems identified by the people in the grama sabhas. By then, the grant-in-aid for each local body from the state government was also made known. Each local body was to make an assessment of the financial resources available for its annual plan, not only from the state and central government but also what it could raise from its own resources, voluntary labour or donations from the people, financial institutions, and from beneficiaries themselves. A detailed document describing the logic of the final selection of the projects along with its statistical and other annexes constitute the Plan Document of the local body.

Once the plans of the gram panchayats were finalised, the

block and district panchayats prepared their plans taking into consideration the plans and suggestions of the gram panchayats.

Before the District Planning Committee formally approved the plans, the plans and projects were appraised by a team of technical volunteers. Nearly 3000 technical experts, most of whom were retired senior government officials, constituted a Voluntary Technical Corps.

An important feature of Kerala's decentralised planning has been the cascading rounds of training before each phase. Around 600 Key Resource Persons were trained at these state-level programmes, who in turn trained about 15,000 District Resource Persons. At the local level, nearly one lakh Resource Persons were trained. The People's Plan Campaign was perhaps the largest non-formal education campaign in the country. The training programmes continued into the subsequent years, though on a smaller scale by the Kerala Institute of Local Administration (KILA).

With certain modifications, the planning procedures have stabilised. Every local government has been preparing their annual plans without a break for the last 25 years. A major problem had been the time overrun in finalising the plans, which squeezed the time available for implementation. However, the time lag has tended to come down and currently, the plan is also approved along with the budget.

Another distinctive feature of the Kerala decentralisation project is the participatory implementation of the projects. For this purpose, different types of beneficiary committees for schools, hospitals, and other institutions have been promoted, and beneficiary committees encouraged for public works. For accountability, popular monitoring committees and social auditing were encouraged. The normal government manuals do not envisage such large-scale direct participation, and therefore numerous ad hoc orders had to be issued and continuously modified before they were formalised into rules. There were many teething troubles and confusion, but over time, a new grassroots level system emerged and stabilised.

There is a strong similarity in the participatory process of planning from below in both the PPC and in the Latin American Participatory Budgeting (PB). The two key differences between them are that in the latter popular participation was limited to planning and did not involve massive training programmes as in the PPC. Given the similarities in the independently evolved experiments in two distant continents, Marta Harnecker tried to develop a synthesis of the two in the concrete context of Venezuela (Harnecker and Bartolome, 2019). The planning from below was an essential component of President Hugo Chávez's '21st-century socialism' (Harnecker, 2015, p. 60).

## THE BALANCE SHEET OF DECENTRALISATION: THE OUTCOMES

Before the achievements of PPC could be consolidated and institutionalised, the Left lost power in the state government in 2001. Since then, the decentralisation in Kerala has survived five turnovers of government while remaining essentially intact. In the international decentralisation literature, this fact alone sets the Kerala experience apart. The PPC created an environment that made it politically inexpedient to undermine decentralisation.

As for the three great 'Fs' of decentralisation — devolution of funds, functions, and functionaries — Kerala has not slid back. In the budget of 2020–21, the share of untied funds in the plan is 25.9 per cent of the plan outlay. The total devolution, including non-plan grants and central and state-sponsored schemes, would be more than Rs 20,000, i.e., nearly 20 per cent of the revenue of the state government (Isaac, 2021). There has not been any major erosion of functions that were devolved. On the other hand, recently, the local governments have been assigned a key role in disaster management. Finally, the number of employees under the local governments, including the transferred employees, has more than doubled. Kerala has continuously been in the front rank on the index of decentralisation prepared for the Union Government.

The basic architecture of the planning from below and the Implementation procedures have remained intact. The campaign mode of popular mobilisation was dismantled by the new UDF government that came to power in 2001. This has been one of the factors for weakening the level of participation in gram sabhas and the planning process. It also adversely affected the pace of institutionalisation of the processes and the ideals generated by the movement.

Twenty-five years is a long enough time span to look back and make a frank assessment of the achievements of this rare experiment in democratic decentralisation in the country. What are the key outcomes?

*Health*

The famed public health system in Kerala was in crisis by the 1990s, confronted with increasing demand for health care arising from a change in the epidemiological regime and a decline in public health expenditure. When the government cut back investments in health, the private sector stepped in to meet the demand-supply gap. The percentage of persons using government facilities in 1986–87 was only 28 per cent (Kannan et al., 1991). The consequence was an escalation of health costs, marginalisation of the poor and inequities in infrastructure, utilisation, and outcomes. The increase in the infant mortality rate from 12 per thousand live births in 1997 to 15 in 2006 was a big embarrassment.

But decentralisation proved to be a turnaround. According to the 71$^{st}$ round of NSSO (2015), the proportion of the population utilising public health services increased to 34 per cent. It has further increased to 48 per cent in the 75$^{th}$ round of NSSO (2018). The IMR has declined to a single digit of 7, lower than the UN

SDG target of 8 in 2020 and far ahead of the national average of 32. Immunisation rates rose to nearly 100 per cent for many diseases (NITI Aayog, 2020).

*Education*

Free and universal school education through the public education system (government schools and private aided schools) slipped below the popular aspiration levels as per capita incomes improved. As a result, the middle class increasingly began to shift towards unaided private schools whose strength increased from 1.5 lakhs students in 1991 to a peak of 4.1 lakhs in 2016–17 (Vimalan, 2019).

The trend has been reversed now, with more than 7.8 lakhs new students in classes 1 to 10, a major portion migrating back from the unaided private sector during the last five years. The number of students in unaided schools has started to decline, and the number of students in the public education system has increased. Kerala has emerged first amongst 20 large states with a score of 76.6 out of 100 in the School Education Quality Index prepared for 2019 (NITI Aayog, 2019).

*Local Roads*

The total road length under the local governments more than doubled from 115306 km in 1995–96 to 231676 km in 2018–19. There has also been a visible improvement in the condition of the town and country roads because of the up-gradation and renovation investment. The roads have become more evenly distributed across districts and regions.

*Housing*

The people of Kerala still remember the One Lakh Housing Scheme of the early 1970s; this scheme provided homes for the beneficiaries of land reforms. But the PPC surprised everyone by constructing 5.7 lakh houses. By the end of the 13th five-year plan in 2022–23, our estimate is that the local governments would have constructed more than 20 lakh houses in the state, which would take Kerala to near-universal housing status.

In 2011, 77 per cent of the houses in the state had drinking water on the premises, while in India, the ratio was 51 per cent. Ninety-five per cent of the houses were electrified as against the national average of 67 per cent. Ninety-five per cent of the houses had latrines, while in India, only 47 per cent of houses had such facilities. Ninety-three per cent of the houses in Kerala had more than one room, while the ratio in India was only 59 per cent (Kannan and Khan, 2016).

*Kudumbasree*

One of the most celebrated outcomes of democratic decentralization has been the emergence and growth of Kudumbasree Neighbourhood Groups (NHGs). They are basically a micro-finance network linked to local governments. They also function as a platform for convergence of anti-poverty programmes, agency for women empowerment, and basic community organisation. At present, there are 2.77 lakh NHGs with a membership of 43 lakh households, each represented by a women member. They have become the most accessible source of microcredit with a fund base of more than Rs . 11,000 crores — Rs 7000 crores from live bank linkage and internal thrift of the NHGs of Rs 4000 crores (Ommen, 2008, Agarwal, 2017, Pat, 2005).

*Poverty Alleviation:* On the eve of the PPC in 1993–94, the poverty ratio was 25.76 and 24.59 per cent in rural and urban areas, respectively. Though not strictly comparable to the earlier series according to Rangarajan Committee Report on Poverty Estimation, in 2011–12, the poverty ratio in Kerala had declined to 7.3 and 5.3 per cent respectively (Kerala State Planning Board, 2016).

In the Multidimensional Poverty Index (MPI), consisting of 10 deprivation indicators related to health, education, and living standards as developed by the UNDP, the proportion of poor in Kerala has declined from 13 per cent to 1 per cent between 2005–06 and 2015–16 (UNDP 2019). Not only is this poverty ratio lowest in India, but also the annual rate of decline of poverty was the highest in the country.

The performance of the local governments has been largely lacklustre on the production front. There are also miles to go for overcoming challenges like participation fatigue, inadequate integration of the plans, nagging corruption, weakness of the tribal sub-plans and so on. Kerala's achievements in decentralisation, however fragile and incomplete, provide a sense of what is possible.

## NEW AGENDA FOR THE LOCAL GOVERNMENTS

The twenty-fifth anniversary of PPC is proving to be an occasion for everyone who has been involved in the decentralisation program to re-evaluate their experience, adopt measures to overcome the weaknesses identified, and set new directions for the democratisation process. The theoretical and legal framework of the practice so far has stood the test of time. However, the institutionalisation of the PPC has not yet been completed. The subsidiary rules have yet to be codified into rules of business of procedure, redeployment of more staff is necessary, and digitalisation of office procedures has to be strengthened.

The key challenge continues to be how to sustain the scale and quality of the participation. The PPC had attempted to overcome the large size barrier to meaningful participation in the grama sabhas by mandating subject group discussions and plenary sessions in the grama sabhas. The solution is to transform the NHGs and residence associations, and other such grassroots community organisations into subsets of the gram sabhas. These micro-groups would discuss the agenda in detail prior to the grama sabha and select representatives to speak at the grama sabha.

The disbanding of the Volunteer Technical Corps by the UDF

government in 2001 was a major setback. The experience so far underlines the need for the incorporation of greater expertise in the local planning process. The grama sabha is the statutory forum, but it is important to promote fora such as different types of management committees for educational, health, and welfare institutions, task forces and committees catering to different levels of expertise and types of aptitude.

Decentralisation has not achieved a significant breakthrough in the material production sectors. A new initiative is to have small-scale industrial clusters at panchayat and municipal levels with the objective of generating annually at least five non-agricultural jobs for every 1000 members of the population. The food program (*Subhiksha Keralama*) has already begun making a visible impact in the production of vegetables, milk, and eggs.

Kerala's poverty alleviation strategy has been characterised by multi-sectoral interventions via different agencies, which were coordinated by the local governments and Kudumbasree. Now it is possible to set the target for eradication of absolute poverty in the state through micro plans for each individual household in extreme poverty. This new program would, to an extent, overcome the earlier failure in addressing the needs of outlier groups such as tribals and fisherfolk.

Despite the gender budgeting and Kudumbasree, gender discrimination and violence against women continues to be a disconcerting feature of social life. A critical review of the gender program is necessary. The proposal for extensive participatory crime mapping of violence against women by each panchayat and municipality and drawing up projects to address the problems identified is indeed an innovative approach that holds much promise.

Kerala's transition to a care economy can be hastened if the already proven geriatric, palliative, differently-abled, and childcare initiatives are scaled up. The target is one Elder Club for every ward, a Buds School for the differently-abled in every locality, smart *anganavadis* and universalisation of palliative care.

After the initial drastic reduction in corruption, its tentacles have been spreading in the past few years. An official review undertaken by M.A. Oommen was sceptical of the efforts to promote beneficiary committees to avoid contractors for implementation of public works (Oommen 2009, p. 85). With this route virtually closed, the solution to corruption lies in ensuring the creation of a transparent and efficient contract system with the option kept open for genuine beneficiary committees to function. A Citizen's Charter has been published by all local governments, but they have not been followed up by social auditing. It is important to legislate a comprehensive Accountability Law.

A major weakness of decentralised planning in Kerala has been the lack of adequate integration in terms of solving local problems or integration of plans of the different tiers of government. With respect to education and health care, a multi-sectoral approach is being adopted by most of the local governments with positive outcomes. On the other hand, watershed planning, so vital for agricultural rejuvenation and solving the drinking water problem, has not yet taken off. The possibilities of launching a campaign, even if not on the scale of 1996, to draw micro watershed programs for land and water management and integrated intervention in the agriculture sector is being explored. A new major activity that has recently been assigned to local governments has been the preparation of local disaster management action plans, for which detailed thematic maps have been prepared for each local government. Both watershed planning and preparation of local disaster management plans can be complementary activities.

The above program has the potential of being converted into a climate change response from below. The mainline of intervention in the sanitation sector has been a reduction in the generation of waste, organic waste processing at the source, collection, and segregation of non-organic waste for recycling or reuse. Localised septage and sewerage treatment plants are necessary to address liquid waste. A major effort to clean up the rivers and canals and plant trees is already being initiated by the local governments.

Right from their launch of the PPC, district plans have been identified as the key instrument for greater integration of the projects of different tiers. Though district plans were prepared in 2000, there were no follow-up actions. The second attempt in 2017 has also not generated the desired impact. The district plan is important not only for integrating the plans of the different tiers through their interaction but also for arriving at a consensus regarding district-level plan guidelines that may be issued by the DPC. Currently, these guidelines are formulated at the state level.

Kerala's democratic decentralisation has expanded the democratic space at the local level. All the new directions that we noted have been experimented by the local initiatives by different local governments and proved successful and, therefore, have come to constitute items in the agenda for scaling-up. Protection and expansion of the democratic space should be the most important objective for the future. Democratic decentralisation does not guarantee any particular outcome. What it promises is that those who desire to create a democratic space intervene and strive for the realisation of their dreams.

Chapter 7

# Nipah, Floods, Landslides, and Covid: The Kerala Alternative

Epidemics, disasters, and calamities test the true leadership, the strength of the political, social, and economic institutions, and social cohesiveness. Starting with the Nipah virus in 2018, the state has faced a natural disaster one after the other up to the present Covid-19 pandemic. It has been widely accepted that these challenges brought out the best in leadership, institutions, and tradition of state-civil society synergy in Kerala. The exemplary success in managing these crises has caught wide attention in the global community. It was indeed an important factor that contributed to the electoral success of the Left in 2021.

The crisis had an important economic fallout. The State Government responded to the consequent economic deterioration through a policy intervention that strengthened the traditional social and welfare expenditures so that the health, education, and social sectors of the state re-emerged with greater vigour.

The crises can be seen as a warning bell of impending climate change and zoonotic health problems. The development policies and programs need to have a greater concern for ecological balance, which, unfortunately, has not been adequately addressed in the past. So, it is certain that the post-crisis period will leave a deep imprint on popular understanding of governmental policies.

## THE FLOODS OF 2018

Kerala experienced abnormally high rainfall from 1 June 2018 to 19 August 2018. This resulted in severe flooding in 13 out of

14 districts in the State. Rainfall over Kerala from 1 to 19 August was 164 per cent higher than the usual precipitation that the state gets during this period. Several places experienced a severe spell of rainfall on 8 and 9 August 2018. Another severe spell started from 14 August and continued till 19 August, resulting in disastrous flooding (Central Water Commission, 2018).

Unusually high rainfall resulted in flash floods, comparable to the flood of 1924 that has been etched in the minds of Keralites as the greatest natural disaster in the region's history. Comparing the two events, researchers were surprised to find that the floodwaters followed very similar contours, areas, and severity though a century divided them. The Indian government declared it a Level 3 Calamity. More than a million people had to be evacuated, more than 480 people died, and the state suffered an economic loss of more than Rs 400 billion.

From 1 August 2018 to 19 August 2018, the total rainfall in Kerala was about 758.6 mm against the normal of 287.6 mm, which was 164 per cent above normal. This unprecedented heavy rainfall filled the capacity of dams, and consequently, 65 per cent of the dams had to be opened, aggravating the flood situation. Dam management became an issue of controversy, but independent hydrological studies undertaken by several premier scientific institutions concluded that it was the heavy rains and not dam management that was at the root of the devastation. This has been substantiated by the Central Water Commission. The Central Water Commission, in its Flood Analysis report in 2018, concluded, 'In a nutshell, it can be concluded that August 2018 flood in Kerala was due to severe storm occurrences during 8–9, August 2018 and 15–17, August 2018. The storm of 15–17 August 2018 resulted in heavy flooding in Periyar, Pamba, Chalakudi and Bharathapuzha sub-basins of Kerala. The rainfall during 15–17, August 2018 was almost comparable to the historical 16–18, July 1924 rainfall of Kerala, particularly in Periyar, Pamba, Chalakudi and Bharatpuzha sub-basins (Central Water Commission, 2018).

The moment the state government realised the scale of the disaster, it swung into action, evacuating the impacted and setting up relief camps. Remarkable coordination of various government departments, particularly revenue, police, health, and local governments, was achieved with the chief minister himself directly taking charge and the ministers deputed to the various districts. The chief minister held evaluation meetings with the districts every day and addressed the people through the media, providing details regarding the flood situation and instructions for the officials. His leadership ensured not only coordination but provided clarity and avoided the usual confusion.

The entire state police, fire, and rescue forces, along with 90 teams of the National Disaster Response Force and three companies of central armed police forces, the central government's 40 helicopters, 31 aircraft, and 18 medical teams were pressed into service. The most important intervention came from more than 4500 fishermen, who deployed more than 650 fishing boats to rescue people from the floodwaters. This fishermen 'army' rescued more than 65,000 marooned people in different districts. Such community actions all over the state were very important in the rescue operations and in containing deaths. Animals were also rescued and transported to special shelters on high rise areas and bridges. Yet nearly 12,000 livestock died.

The local self-governments were given the charge of setting up and running the relief camps with the help of revenue officials. 1.2 million people were registered in these camps during the peak of floods. These camps were excellently managed by the local governments (LSGIs). There were no complaints regarding free food, clothing, and healthcare in these camps. As the floodwaters receded, local teams of volunteers cleaned up mud and waste in the houses, and people were rehabilitated.

Rs 10,000 was paid to every displaced household, compensation of Rs 4 lakh for every house completely destroyed and Rs 10 lakh for those whose houses were destroyed and had to be relocated.

Compensation was paid for agricultural damage, more than what is permitted by central norms. Even while this process was going on, the government declared a program for 'Build Back Better', which included projects for room for the river, rebuilding the roads, bridges, houses and public institutions damaged by the floods.

## THE CASE OF KUTTANAD FLOOD PLAINS

We will not go into all the details, but the case of Kuttanad needs to be narrated. Kuttanadu lies mostly below sea level, and it is a flood plain fed by four major rivers in central Kerala, the rivers Pamba, Mnimala, Achenkovil, and Meenachil. Out of 1.63 Billion Cubic Metres (BCM), the runoff generated during the 15 to 17 August 2018 rainfall, only about 0.6 BCM runoff could drain out of the Vembanadu lake. The remaining runoff volume of about 1 BCM created the rise of the water level in the lake and nearby areas. This heavy spell of rain and runoff through the rivers discharging to Vembanadu totally inundated the entire Kuttanadu catchment. So, it is an appropriate illustrative case study (Central Water Commission, 2018). In a matter of two days from August 15, the entire population of 50,000 families from the region was evacuated, temporarily putting them up in relief camps set up in schools and colleges. When the water level receded after a fortnight, they were to be rehabilitated after cleaning up the houses and premises.

Rescuing the inhabitants from the inundated flood plain was a hectic task. Initially, people moved out through the roads, but by evening, road traffic was closed in most parts due to rising floodwaters. Panic set in. A fleet of high-rise Taurus trucks was pushed into service to evacuate the people who were gathered on bridges and high-rise land patches and in some parts of the roads on the night of August 16. Available water transport ferried people to the nearby towns. But the water transport became very difficult because commercial boats could not transverse under the bridges whose clearances were considerably reduced due to the water level rise. It is here that the marine fishermen volunteers, and their boats became saviours. They were transported from the seacoast to the backwaters, and they could operate through the flooded lanes and walled compounds. The outcome was that the entire population was evacuated within two days and one night without a single mishap.

The entire coordination was done at the district headquarters, where a war room had been set up. Volunteers, some of them IT specialists, also setup a call centre which carried out effective information exchange. A city college building was converted into a warehouse and distribution centre for food grains and other essential articles. Donations, both in cash and kinds, were pouring in. The warehouse and distribution centre was working under the supervision of senior government officials.

The relief camps were operated by the concerned local governments, which they carried out with empathy and efficiency. Common kitchen, efficient septage removal with mechanical suckers, hygiene, distribution of clothes and medical facilities characterised the camps. Though the government cancelled all official Onam celebrations, the relief camps were in a festive mood with traditional feasts, games, music, dance, and competitions for children.

A small incident that the author experienced brought home powerfully the transformation of the local governments. A foreign delegation that visited a major relief camp was so impressed with the festive look of the camp that they asked me to introduce them to the NGO that was running the camp. I pointed to the woman panchayat president standing in the crowd. The local government at the cutting edge was acting like a non-governmental organisation mobilising the synergy of working with the people. It indeed was an important objective of democratic decentralisation.

An emergency program for rebuilding roads and houses was

implemented after a quick digital survey. Besides support from the state government, a social media campaign styled 'I am with Alleppey' mobilised large donations in money and kind, which were used for rehabilitation activities.

A long run program for flood mitigation and eco-restoration was also drawn up: modernisation of the regulatory barrage and spillway built in the 1970s, desilting the lake to enhance the water carrying capacity, strengthening the bunds of paddy fields, and a livelihood promotion program. This programme, announced in the budget as the Second Kuttanad Package, is being currently implemented (Kerala State Planning Board, 2019a).

## 2019 KERALA FLOODS AND LANDSLIDES

August 2019 appeared to be a repetition of the events of the previous year, though with less intensity, with heavy rains from August 8. Most of the state was placed under a red alert. The drastic feature of this second flood was that we had 80 landslides in a span of two days, particularly in the northern districts. The rainfall was accompanied by a sea surge. One hundred twenty-one persons died, and lakhs of people were displaced who were moved to relief camps. The landslides were precisely in danger-prone hill areas identified by scientists because of environmental degradation and potential soil piping areas.

It was evident that the rebuild programme of the state must be sensitive to eco-restoration. A major limitation was the lack of financial resources. There was a generous response to an appeal for donations to the Chief Minister's Disaster Relief Fund (CMDRF), which collected around Rs 4700 crores. Unfortunately, the government of India declined permission to accept offers of support from foreign governments, particularly the Gulf countries with whom Kerala has centuries of warm relations and is the destination for more than 2 million Malayali migrant workers. Such a stance from the Union Government would have been understandable if its financial support from Delhi had been sufficient. Apart from the normal State Disaster Relief Fund (SDRF) contributions, the central aid was paltry. Kerala was forced to take long-term loans from multi-lateral agencies for its rebuilding programmes. These were required to stay within the normal 3 per cent of GDP borrowing envelope and therefore provided no additional resources. Worse still, the Union Government refused to provide any additional support for the 2019 floods.

## FLATTENING THE COVID CURVE IN THE FIRST WAVE

Before the floods, in May 2018, the deadly Nipah epidemic broke out in northern Kerala. Seventeen out of 18 Nipah infected patients died. It was indeed an occasion that demonstrated the robustness of the Kerala health system. The highly dreaded epidemic has been stamped out, containing it at the local level itself. Health workers were trained to safely trace, track, and transport persons with symptoms. Isolation beds and protocols for providing supportive care were in place, and people became familiar with the importance of observing house quarantine. The learning and experiences gained from the successful containment of the deadly epidemic helped Kerala formulate a strategy and protocol to manage the Covid-19 pandemic swiftly.

As soon as news of the epidemic in Wuhan hit the headlines in January 2020, Kerala began to make systematic preparations. The standard operating procedures issued by the state covered, among other things, infection prevention and control, deployment of ambulances, biomedical waste management, body fluids spill management, disinfection and sterilisation, hand washing, protocols for cremating/ burying dead bodies, use of Personal Protection Equipment (PPE), sample collection and transportation. A set of comprehensive guidelines covering testing, quarantine, hospital admissions, treatment and discharge was also issued and has been revised often to accommodate and cope with the updated understanding and strategies. The guidelines were accompanied by training modules for health workers and volunteers.

## HEALTH STRATEGY

The first three positive Covid cases in Kerala were from students who had returned from Wuhan. Since all arrivals from Wuhan were quarantined, the further spread was successfully prevented. These three cases recovered from Covid by 20 February, and the state remained Covid-free till 9 March.

The dynamics of tracing and tracking changed when new epicentres opened in Europe, Iran, and the Gulf Co-operation Council (GCC) countries. Many migrant workers living in these countries returned to Kerala. Kerala continued to track the returnees, now much more significant in number — who remained in quarantine and tracked their contacts. Soon positive cases started emerging from this cohort, and Kerala emerged as the state with the largest Coronavirus (COVID-19) patients in India.

Many simulations about the likely spread of the pandemic predicted a dire situation for Kerala. An exercise was undertaken by Protiviti (2020) for Times Network on 12 April 2020, estimated that infections would peak in Kerala on 8 May with 72,057 cases, with 22,281 severe cases requiring intensive care. However, the actual numbers turned out to be just a few dozens.

What helped Kerala was the aggressive strategy of quarantining/placing under observation everyone arriving from outside hot spots and testing all symptomatic persons. If tested positive, contacts were traced, and these people were placed under observation. The number of new persons placed in institutional or home quarantine began to sharply increase from 495 cases in the first week of March to 84,718 patients in the last week of the same month. It peaked on 4 April with 1,71,355 persons under observation. After that, the number steadily fell with a decline in the number of new persons put under observation during April.

The number of persons tested as a proportion of the persons quarantined remained low till the second week of April since adequate testing kits were not available. The number of persons under quarantine or observation increased as Kerala started community surveillance. An important point to be noted is that almost all the positive cases were from people under observation. So, community spread was effectively prevented, even though the strategy of testing only symptomatic persons from among the contacts would have missed asymptomatic contacts who were on observation. Such asymptomatic cases, even if undetected, would not lead to spread for the simple reason that the quarantine period would have neutralised the infectious period. The fact that positive cases remained low, even after the number of tests among the non-contact general public has been scaled up, is a testimonial to the state's effective prevention strategy. Kerala's strategy of quarantining all travellers from epicentres of the disease cost the state revenue from tourism but has paid off in the number of potential infections averted.

The Covid curve continued to gain momentum through March 2020. April marked the steady decline in new positive cases and accelerated recoveries. As a result, the Covid Curve lost momentum, and Kerala flattened the curve of Covid-19 infections. As per the first seroprevalence survey in 2020, the percentage of persons with antibodies in Kerala was only 11 per cent, as against the national average of 20. The same relative situation continued during the second seroprevalence survey, the ratio being 44 per cent in Kerala as against the national average of 68 per cent.

The core of Kerala's Covid response was its public health system. The preparedness and additional investment in health infrastructure that substantially improved the health care facilities have boosted health workers' morale, which is a sharp contrast to the sense of helplessness and unrest among health workers in many of even the elite medical centres in India. The government has borne the entire cost of testing and treating COVID-19 in the state.

From the beginning, the health minister of Kerala, K.K. Shailaja, who led the Nipah response from the front, provided visible and robust leadership to the health department. The competence demonstrated by the effective containment of the Nipah outbreak and management of two successive floods helped the health care system achieve a high degree of confidence in dealing with the epidemic. This also created an outstanding level of people's trust in the government health system.

## HUMANE LOCKDOWN AND PUBLIC TRUST

Kerala declared a lockdown even before the national lockdown but with a two-day notice. This advanced information helped the people prepare to meet such a situation unheard of in the region. During the lockdown, a Covid package of Rs 20000 crores half of which was essentially direct income transfer to the people through liquidation of welfare arrears and advance payments and consumption loans through Kudumbasree microfinance, was announced and implemented. The financing was primarily done through front-loading the public borrowings.

The government ensured that nobody would go hungry in Kerala: food kits were distributed every month apart from grains distributed through the public distribution system. All local governments opened community kitchens serving more than five lakh meals per day at its peak. Food was delivered to the homes of people who could not come to the kitchen.

Crisis times give room for a lot of misinformation. The government's constant efforts to communicate with the people increased transparency and trust in the system. The Chief Minister of Kerala, Pinarayi Vijayan, after reviewing the data and discussing policy decisions, shared important information with the people every day through a live press conference which became the most-watched event in those days in Kerala. Media, both mainstream and new, have continuously communicated with the people, though some of them were providing misleading or false information.

Prompt response, constant communication, and updates helped the government earn the public trust and co-operation to tackle the task though it has been tough. They believed that their government is transparent, sharing truthful information and that it will take care of them should they fall sick and support them if they need it. In return, they were prepared to adhere to the restrictions the government imposed to control the epidemic. Messages on social distancing and self-quarantine were viewed seriously by the people, and they also exercised peer pressure on errant persons.

## LOCAL GOVERNMENTS

Local Government (LGs) interventions in improving the health infrastructure; role in the purchase of drugs and medical equipment; employment of additional doctors, nurses and paramedical staff on contract; and supplementing the honorarium of ASHA (Accredited Social Health Activist) workers have been narrated in chapter 6. They also connect the civil society organisations such as palliative care organisations, voluntary food programs, and Kudumbasree health volunteers with the health department. They play an essential role in geriatric care, support differently-abled, and finance special schools for children with cognitive disabilities. They oversee the prevention of vector and waterborne infectious diseases. Given the high level of involvement of local governments in health and related sectors, it was only natural that they played an essential role in the fight against COVID-19.

Local government involvement was formalised through a government order on 20 March 2020. Local Governments created awareness about COVID-19, the Break the Chain movement, and sanitation; provided support for persons in isolation; and ensured availability of essential items. The documentation for prevention efforts, including inventorying medical and other resources, the number of persons in need of additional support, etc., has been the responsibility of local governments.

The community kitchens provided food to anyone who needed it. These kitchens sprang up in less than three days across the state, which brought out the strength of the local governments beyond the formal assignments. Besides these community kitchens, more than 1000 budget hotels were opened and operated by Kudumbasree. There were also palliative care groups that provided free food at the doorsteps of destitute bedridden persons.

All persons above 65 and those suffering from chronic diseases were asked to stay indoors and, if necessary, in the isolation rooms in the houses since they are at higher risk of adverse consequences if infected. It was a daunting task for Kerala, with 13.5 per cent of the population above the age of 65 and a high incidence of diabetes and hypertension. Many local governments effectively implemented this reverse quarantining of more than 40 lakh people in the houses, contributing to relatively low caseload among the elderly and low fatality rate.

Yet another responsibility of the local government has been monitoring the camps of migrant workers and ensuring their food and medical treatment. Kerala accounted for 65 per cent of the 23567 camps and 47 per cent of the 6.5 lakhs migrant workers sheltered in them in India during the national lockdown.

The local government representatives and officials visited the camps, checked sanitation, provided food kits in some locations, and in some cases even made available free mobile chargers and even chess and carom boards to keep them engaged. An interesting and good practice is that of Uralunkal Labour Contract Cooperative Society, the largest construction cooperative in India with nearly 3000 workers, most of whom are migrant workers. The migrant workers are encouraged to take membership in the society so that they get the full benefit of a member (Isaac and Williams, 2017). When the crisis came, those workers who wanted to return home were sent back at the expense of the cooperative itself in special buses. While the situation of the migrant workers is far from satisfactory, the local governments tried their best to make the lockdown period as bearable as possible.

In addition to health and local self-government departments, departments such as police, disaster management, education, and a few other departments also issued similar guidelines to support COVID-19 prevention efforts. These guidelines would not have produced the desired results if their implementation was not coordinated and appropriately monitored, a task which the Chief Minister himself shouldered.

## OPPOSITION AGITATIONS AND EROSION OF PUBLIC TRUST AND CONSENSUS

The all-around appreciation in containing the initial entry of the virus by students returning from Wuhan unnerved the opposition. The initial forays were academic in nature, challenging the containment strategy of the government on the floor of the legislature and proposing an alternative mitigation strategy. But the latter strategy has a high cost of avoidable deaths and post Covid ailments. Therefore, there were hardly any takers for the alternative suggested.

The first major confrontation took place around entry policy regarding non-resident Keralites returning to the state. The non-resident Keralites wanted to return or send their families back to Kerala, which appeared to be a haven. In fact, the Kerala assembly in April 2020 passed a unanimous resolution against the Ministry of External Affairs (MoEA) that have placed stringent restrictions on NRI returnees. But Kerala government laid down its own strict procedures for returning migrants. They had to register on a Kerala portal, and if they did not have a Covid negative certificate, they needed to undergo multilayer screening at the airport and compulsory quarantining at home or in hotels. There was much confusion because the central government registration portal was not integrated with the Kerala portal, and information was available only with the arrival of the aircraft. All these confusions provided much fodder for the opposition's criticism.

The confrontation broke into open hostility at the border road check posts, where there was much delay as many people were returning without registering in the Kerala portal. A group of opposition leaders tried to force the entry of the return migrants without completing the formalities. There was also confusion at the railway stations where trains arrived without adequate notice and with unregistered passengers.

The result was a surge in the cases, most of them from contact within Kerala rather than imported from outside. By July, it was evident that community spread was taking place in certain pockets, particularly in coastal areas. Police imposed stringent restrictions to isolate such areas, leading to violence in a Thiruvananthapuram coastal village. With the community spread, the strategy of testing, tracing, and isolating was difficult, and the government decided to give a greater responsibility to police in monitoring, tracing, and surveillance. This immediately gave rise to criticism against police raj, the surveillance state, and withdrawal from the participatory approach.

Against this background, the controversy regarding the selection of a non-resident Malayalee owned tech-firm, Sprinklr, for Covid big data analysis became the focal point of the media. Sprinklr was a consultant to the World Health Organisation (WHO) for big data analysis. Kerala was aiming to use a large body of health information on Kerala households collected by WHO in previous decades, along with data being generated regarding quarantined and hospitalised people due to Covid in the state. Sprinklr was willing to provide the service for free for the first year and ready to accept conditions for data privacy, including hosting the data at the earliest on an Indian server.

The opposition created a vicious controversy regarding lapses in the procedure, data privacy, and then finally corruption. It was argued that the tasks could be undertaken by state or central IT agencies. It was obvious that the critics overestimated the big data analytics capability and ability to provide the results within the crucial timeframe of the existing agencies. Nevertheless, they succeeded in generating a cloud of suspicion, and the government shelved the programme, which was important for meeting the inevitable new wave of Covid.

It was at this juncture that the Gold Smuggling scandal broke out. It involved the smuggling of gold by a gang linked to the United Arab Emirates Consulate, with one among them closely associated with a high official in the Chief Minister's office. The high voltage story became the theme of endless evening prime time TV discussions, the main story in the print media, and a topic of aggressive protest mobilisation by the opposition, flouting Covid norms. The entry of the central investigative agencies (Customs, CBI, and ED) provided a daily dose of stories to keep the media circus and agitations going.

Yet another corruption controversy erupted. Now an allegation about the Life Mission sub-project subcontract given by the donors for the construction of flats with the funds of Red Crescent added fuel to the fire.

Despite all these raked up controversies, the LDF won a handsome victory in the local government election in November 2020. With this defeat, the desperate opposition stuck even more viciously to the road of confrontation with their propaganda and agitations.

Most of the electorate rejected the allegations against the government, and even some who were inclined to agree with them were appreciative of the government's Covid response. But it was evident that the public consensus had evaporated, and there was a dent in public trust.

Under this socio-political environment, Kerala entered a three-month-long campaign for the state legislative assembly elections. The norms for social distancing and other Covid protocol could not be fully complied with during the intense election campaign with house-to-house visits and public rallies. As a result, we found that the caseload rose during the election period and merged with the second country-wide wave of Covid.

## THE CURIOUS CASE OF THE COVID SECOND WAVE

The curious case of Kerala was that while in the country the second wave of Covid began to decline from the second week of May, the caseload in Kerala started to rise from the end of June, peaking at the end of July with more than 32,000 new cases and accounting for nearly 70 per cent of the caseload in India at the beginning of September. The states positivity rate continued to hover around 15 to 17 per cent. Some have suggested that the Delta variant might have arrived late in Kerala. Or it might be the case that fatigue was setting in the health personnel and even the public. Whatever be the precise reason, the Kerala Covid surge was politicised at the national level by the BJP to run down the Kerala model.

Though the higher caseload in Kerala is indisputable, conclusions of interstate comparisons must be taken with caution. The under-reporting of the infection in India is widespread, as proved by the latest seroprevalence survey. Comparing the estimated number of cases from the antibody prevalence rate and the actual cases reported in December shows that while only 1 in 30 cases is reported in India, the ratio is 1 in 6 cases in Kerala. The prevalence of antibodies is 43 per cent in the Kerala sample as against 64 per cent at the national level. It also implies that the potentially vulnerable population in Kerala is much larger at this point than the rest in India, and with the Delta variant and increased mobility of people.

The solution to the infection lies in ramping up the vaccination rate, which is not within the state government's control. The vaccine supply by the central government has been much below the demand, and therefore the vaccination programme has been progressing at a slow pace. Yet, Kerala would still have the highest proportion of people vaccinated. And it was the state with the least vaccine wastage.

Comparing the second-wave experience in Kerala and the national level would still be instructive. The national scene was characterised by confusion, conflicting authorities, lack of oxygen hospital beds, and apoplectic scenes of floating bodies and mass funeral pyres. The Kerala scenario, despite high test positivity, was a sharp contrast. Kerala ensured that the hospital capacity, ICU beds, oxygen supply and other facilities were never overwhelmed by the Covid surge. New Covid hospital wards were set up. First Line Covid Treatment Centres expanded, and domiciliary care centres opened.

The results can be seen in low fatality rates in the state. Despite the sharp increase in the second wave, the fatality rate in Kerala is at 0.5, nearly one-third of the national ratio of 1.4. The opposition has been making much noise around the norms for inclusion in the Covid death count. Kerala has been following the norms set by the central government. Even if it is modified for whatever reason, it is not going to make any fundamental change in the scenario. Though we will have to wait for the next census to estimate the excess deaths, on the basis of the sample death registration data, it has been revealed that the extent of under-reporting in Kerala is relatively very low. The multiple of excess data to reported Covid death is less than 1.6 in Kerala, while for India, the ratio is 5.8. (Hindu Data Team, 2021; Srinivasan Ramani, 2021).

Given the prolonged strains to livelihood and general fatigue from state-wide, lockdowns and severe restrictions on mobility would have to be relaxed. Therefore, a modified strategy of localised mobility restrictions depending upon the severity of the infection and close watch on the capacity of health facilities with the total caseload was adopted. Meanwhile, every effort was made to accelerate the vaccination process.

### THE KERALA EXIT STRATEGY

Kerala prepared an exit strategy for the economy from Covid restrictions. Even under the Covid conditions, agriculture and allied sectors and cottage and small-scale industry had been opened. Perhaps the Covid-19 crisis may provide an opportunity to reverse the trend of decline in paddy and intercrop cultivation in garden lands.

The Peoples' Plan Campaign had succeeded in establishing many aggregation models of participatory small-scale vegetable cultivation. The Agriculture Department drew up a comprehensive package for agrarian revival in collaboration with the local governments. Reopening of the traditional industries will be paralleled with a programme promoting new enterprises. The target is to generate five new jobs in the non-agriculture sector for every 1000 persons in every local government area.

The MGNREGS was frontloaded to the maximum extent to provide employment and income to the poor, focusing on de-silting and reconstructing about half the 80000 km canal network in Kerala, which would help to mitigate the possible floods during monsoon and help irrigation in summer. The gram panchayats are the sole agency for implementing the MGNREGS works in Kerala, and a convergence approach with the local plan was adopted. A massive fruit tree planting program was also declared.

Unlocking the economy is a much larger exercise than local agriculture and industry programmes. It would require concerted action from the Central and State Governments. The state has already drawn up certain priority sectors such as pharmaceuticals and medical devices industries, biotechnology and information technology sectors, value-adding agro-processing industries and tourism. The new brand image the state has gained as a safe and resilient region would be utilised to attract investment to these sectors. The branding also become important in opening the tourism sector. With the expected heavy return migration, special efforts would also have to be made for the rehabilitation and reintegration of migrants.

The Budget of 2021–22 had also outlined a strategy for transforming the economic base of the state by integrating innovation and modern technology with a focus on knowledge-intensive industries. We will discuss the strategy for a transition to the knowledge economy in chapter 9.

Large-scale infrastructure investment from resources mobilised through special purpose vehicles like the Kerala Infrastructure Investment Fund Board (KIIFB) will also be playing the role of the stimulus package for the regional economy and an important component of the exit strategy. We will take up this infrastructure investment program in the next chapter.

Chapter 8

# Addressing the Infrastructural Deficit: Kerala Infrastructure Investment Fund Board (KIIFB)

Kerala has been woefully backward in infrastructure development. Its transport system has virtually degenerated into a mono-mode road transport network, whose quality is one of the poorest in the country with no six-lane roads, numerous rail crossings, and old bridges. With one of the highest densities of cars in the country, the highways are clogged and accident-prone. Waterways, the primary mode of transportation in Kerala up to the 1950s, have fallen to disuse due to lack of modernisation. The catchment area of Kochi, the only major port, has steadily been encroached on by new ports of the neighbouring states. Capacity addition in electricity generation has been meagre during the last quarter of a century, the transmission lines limited to 220 kV and weak distribution network. The industrial parks are mostly 1970s vintage, and new modern thematic parks lag behind the other states. The school and hospital infrastructure are inadequate, and good stadiums and theatres are exceptions.

The above backwardness reflected a low public investment in infrastructure. There was hardly any balance left for infrastructure investment after the social welfare expenditure, salaries, pensions, and interest. From the 1980s, the state has been on a continuous revenue deficit, i.e., a significant portion of the capital receipts of the state is also spent on revenue expenditure. As a result, the capital expenditure to GSDP in the state from the 1980s has been only around half the national average (see Table 5.3).

The fiscal trend from 2001 has been broadly towards greater consolidation, and the revenue deficit has tended to come down until the Covid-19 epidemic of 2020–21. However, with avenues of resource mobilisation constrained by the loss of independent taxation powers after the introduction of GST, it is challenging for Kerala to envisage eliminating revenue deficit altogether like most other states because of the committed social sector expenditure. How can the state government overcome the infrastructure deficit that has become a serious barrier to investment and growth in such a situation?

Obviously, it cannot be from the budget alone because the state governments must comply with the Fiscal Responsibility and Budget Management (FRBM) Acts, limiting the state's annual borrowing to 3 per cent of GSDP. Further, constitutionally, any public borrowing by a state government can be done only with the central government's authorisation. The public investment for infrastructure would have to come from outside the budget. Borrowing by public sector units (PSUs) or government financial institutions is not considered a part of the government borrowing if the borrowed funds do not enter government accounts. This was the only path Kerala could adopt to overcome its historical backwardness in infrastructure.

## KIIFB: INCREASING ANNUITY MODEL

Mobilising resources through Special Purpose Vehicles (SPV) is not something new. All state governments and the central government set up SPVs to implement large-scale revenue-earning infrastructural projects. The lenders examine the project's financial viability, and their degree of comfort is enhanced by extending the government guarantee for the loan. However, this mode of resource mobilisation can be adopted only for revenue-earning projects. What about other infrastructure projects that may not be revenue-generating?

In such cases, many state governments utilise an annuity scheme of financing. Annuity-based funding through public-private partnerships (PPP) has been adopted as a powerful mechanism for enhancing capital investment in a country or region. In this scheme, as the owner of the newly created public infrastructure, the government undertakes to make a fixed/ variable payment, viz. annuity, to the project implementation agency, over a period to meet the project's cost. The annuity is agreed upon through a competitive bidding process. The annuity may be a predetermined budgetary allocation if the implementing agency is a public company or a statutory body. The hybrid annuity scheme is the model in which the government needs to make a partial up-front payment to reduce the cost. This is the usual model used by the National Highway Authority of India (NHAI). As of December 2019, the central government has taken up 93 projects of Rs 87292 crores under both these schemes. The state governments have taken up 81 schemes of Rs 9701 crores.

The Kerala experience with annuity schemes of financing has not been encouraging. Competition in bidding is usually limited, resulting in high costs since the implementing agencies must raise the resources. An evaluation of the scheme revealed that the implicit interest rate is 15 per cent or higher. Given this situation, the government of Kerala decided to convert the Kerala Infrastructure Investment Fund Board (KIIFB), a dormant public financial institution, into a statutory corporate body to mobilise resources for a bundle of projects approved by the government. The government agreed to pay an annuity of 50 per cent of the motor vehicles tax and cess on petrol to KIIFB. In other words, the annuity would increase every year depending upon the tax buoyancy. So KIIFB can be described as a 'growing annuity scheme'.

A question remains: how can one be sure that the annuity payment and repayments received from revenue-earning projects would be sufficient for the repayment of the debt and interest? How can the liquidity of the entity be ensured so that payment is always made? In other words, how can the inflows and outflows be matched at any point in time so that the KIIFB does not face any liquidity problem? The answer lies in the Controlled Leverage Model (CLM) on which the operation of KIIFB is based.

The elaborate database of KIIFB consists of all the details of the inflows like budgetary allocations, funds raised from the market, receipts from revenue-generating projects, and outflows like project pay-outs and debt servicing. KIIFB has developed its Asset liability Management Model (ALM). This model has predictive analytics and relies on Artificial Intelligence/Machine Learning. It enables KIIFB to predict, among other things, how assets and liabilities will match at any point in time within the project horizon. At no point in time will the liabilities exceed the assets. The projects would be taken up only within this self-imposed constraint. Therefore, the question of KIIFB's liabilities boomeranging to the government as direct liabilities does not arise as long as the government complies with the annuity it is legally bound to pay.

### KIIFB'S STRUCTURE — CHECKS AND BALANCES

The idea of a government-corporate body mobilising funds from the open market creating transport infrastructure worth Rs 40,000 crores was unveiled in the last budget of the 2006–11 LDF government. The opposition greeted the proposal with derision, and the next UDF government shelved it until their last year's budgets. Nothing happened other than the reference in the budget. Learning from this experience, the new Left government in 2016 firmly placed it on the agenda in their first budget. It was announced that instead of setting up a new company, the KIIFB established by the then LDF government in 1999 would be resurrected and revamped. So, a comprehensive amendment to the KIIFB Act of 1999 was moved and was unanimously adopted by the legislative assembly in 2016.

*Resource Mobilisation*

The first objective was to make KIIFB borrowings compliant with the Financial Responsibility and Budget Management (FRBM) Act. The funds mobilised by KIIFB were earlier deposited in the treasury. The consequence was that the debt was used to service the current expenditure, and it became a dead burden. Now statutorily, no part of the KIIFB borrowings can be deposited in the treasury or used for budgetary purposes.

The amendments ensured that 50 per cent of the motor vehicles tax and the cess on petrol would annually be given as grants to KIIFB. In a sense, KIIFB is only securitising future income flows. As an added assurance to the investors, the government guarantees the repayment of loans. The remunerative projects, including land acquisitions, would have to be paid back from their future revenues.

The new law also enhanced the scope of fundraising of the KIIFB from traditional general obligation bonds and term loans from financial institutions to include revenue bonds, land bonds, and new innovative financing structures permitted by the RBI and SEBI.

*Procedures for Implementation*

Fears were expressed that the KIIFB might emerge as a parallel government abrogating the powers of the various departments since the money does not come into the treasury. This fear was unfounded. The KIIFB is only a financial institution for mobilising funds. The KIIFB finances the projects declared in the budget speech or decided by the cabinet. Procedures have been laid down for the departments to identify their special purpose vehicles to prepare the Detailed Project Report (DPR). Works are awarded through an open bid process. Once the KIIFB board approves the DPR after careful vetting, its role is to transfer funds to the contractors as authorised by the concerned SPV.

Of course, the KIIFB would independently monitor the

implementation through an Inspection Authority to ensure total compliance with the approved plan. It also may be noted that almost all departments had their own SPVs. Thus, for example, Public Works Department (PWD) had Kerala Road Fund Board, Kerala Roads and Bridges Corporation, and Kerala State Construction Corporation. Projects approved by the legislature or decided at the cabinet are executed through these unique arms of different departments. The KIIFB is financing the projects after carefully studying the viability and monitoring the adherence of project implementation to the approved parameters. This is the statutory position regarding projects. There will be no difference to the existing procedures of implementation and supervision and, therefore, no infringement on the rights of the departments.

*Organisational Structure*

The KIIFB is headed by the Chief Minister, the chairman of the Director Board. There is also an executive committee headed by the finance minister, which looks after the day-to-day affairs. There is also a Fidelity Trust and Advisory Commission (FTAC) of eminent experts with impeccable credentials who have a watchdog function and certify that the funds have not been misused.

A robust accountability mechanism has also been instituted. Besides statutory auditing and international standard peer auditing, there is also an audit by the Accountant General (AG). The AG's report and the FTAC's fidelity certificates are placed before the assembly and are scrutinised by relevant legislative committees. Though the receipts and expenditure of these projects financed by KIIFB are not part of the government accounts and therefore not part of the budget, since they are announced in the budget speech, the legislators have the opportunity to discuss them thoroughly.

## THE PERFORMANCE OF KIIFB 2016–2021

At the end of the financial year 2020–21, KIIFB had sanctioned

821 projects worth Rs 40100 crores. Apart from this, the KIIFB has approved projects worth Rs 20000 crores for land acquisition for industrial parks, national highways, and railways. Thus, the total outlay of the projects supported by the KIIFB comes to over Rs 60,000 crores. Besides, around Rs10,000 crores projects are declared in the budgets still under different stages of project preparation. Of the total projects approved, projects worth Rs 19,100 crores have been tendered or are being implemented. It is expected that most of the projects will be completed in 3 years.

*Transport*

The most significant component of the approved projects is road connectivity — 2,985 Km of designed roads, 10 by-passes extending to 43 Kms, 20 Flyovers over 22 Kms, 74 bridges over 53 Kms. The total estimated cost of these projects works out to be Rs18,000 crores. Most of the projects under DPR preparation are related to road connectivity, particularly flyovers and bridges. The largest among the road projects are the north-south Hill Highway and Coastal Highway. An exciting feature of the Hill Highway has been the free surrender of land by the concerned landholders and simultaneous construction taking place at different stretches of the road. The Coastal Highway has a pedestrian and a cycle track, and it connects all the coastal tourist centres. However, the project has been beset with problems associated with land availability.

The KIIFB has adopted high standards for its roads adhering to the norms of the Indian Road Congress. Transportation safety, amenities for pedestrians, drainage, and long-term maintenance are among the prominent features of KIIFB roads. Even though the initial cost of these roads would be substantially higher, the maintenance cost will be lower in the long term, and it will have a longer life. The speciality of these designer roads is the adoption of modern technologies such as full-depth reclamation, cold recycling, and geo-textiles.

The strategy is not merely about expanding the road network

but also the diversification of the transport system. The most critical intervention is the north-south waterway from Kovalam to Bekal. KIIFB also contributes to Kochi's urban transport and various inland water networks. KIIFB also contributes to the land acquisition cost of new rail projects, particularly to the arterial highspeed rail corridor.

*Power and Drinking Water*

With more than Rs5000 crores allocation, the power sector is the second most important sector after transportation. Kerala is deficient in power generation and remains dependent upon purchase from the national grid. But the state has been handicapped by the lack of a high-tension arterial transmission line. Trans-grid 2.0, 400 kV transmission backbone financed by the KIIFB, ensures that electricity supply needs up to the year 2040 are met. Yet another game-changer is the K-Fon project that would provide an alternative internet superhighway using electricity poles and linking all the public institutions and households in Kerala.

The KIIFB investment in drinking water projects comes to around Rs . 5000 crores. The Kerala Water Authority is undertaking 87 large and integrated drinking water projects. They include new source-based projects as well as replacing the dilapidated pipe network to reduce leakage and improve the quality of water. They would create 1600 MLD capacity and 2500 km distribution pipeline cover nearly one crore consumers.

*Social Sectors*

Education and healthcare infrastructure has been upgraded through nearly 250 projects at the cost of more than Rs 8000 crores. The digitalization of school classrooms has been completed, and that of colleges is ongoing. Comprehensive up-gradation of the physical infrastructure of government educational institutions includes 57 lakh sq. feet of new school buildings, 33 lakh sq. feet of university and college buildings, and 5 lakh sq. feet of IT buildings. The up-gradation of hostels and model schools of the SC/ST department is also being taken up.

The KIIFB funding in The health sector has been focused on the tertiary health sector, such as medical colleges, super speciality hospitals, and district hospitals. The KIIFB is also supporting several taluk hospitals. Apart from 46 lakh sq. feet of hospital buildings, most modern dialysis units, cardiology, oncology facilities and equipment are acquired with the KIIFB assistance. Projects costing Rs 2000 crores are under preparation for the educational and health sectors.

The KIIFB projects also include infrastructure in agriculture, fisheries, forest, and some selected departmental buildings. To the surprise of many, KIIFB is financing Rs40 to 50 crores cultural complexes in every district and 44 Stadiums having a built-up area of 37 lakh sq. feet. The rationale is that as Kerala's per capita income improves rapidly, there should be such cultural and sports avenues to guard against consumerist culture.

*Other Mega Projects*

Many mega infrastructure projects are being kick-started from the KIIFB pooled fund facility for land acquisitions in transportation and industrial infrastructure. The K-rail, a 530 km long semi high-speed rail connecting Thiruvananthapuram in the south and Kasaragod in the north, is an ambitious project to reduce the present travel time by road by three-fourths and wean away long-distance car travellers to the public transport system. Its projected cost is Rs 63,000 crores and is to be implemented as a joint venture of Indian railways and the Kerala government. Besides the K-rail, the NH widening, and Industrial corridors, among others, are getting realised with the KIIFB support for the initial land cost.

The Kochi–Palakkad High Tech Industrial Corridor has been approved by the Central Government as part of the Chennai–Bangalore Industrial Corridor. This will have an investment of Rs10,000 crores and will provide 22,000 direct employment opportunities. Steps are being taken to acquire 2321 acres of land in Palakkad and Kochi. In the first phase, a hub of high-tech services and finance, namely the Global Industrial Finance and Trade City (GIFT City), will be set up on 220 hectares of land. Another one is the Kochi–Mangalore Industrial Corridor which will be a big shot in the arm for the development of the Malabar region. The master plan for this must be prepared. The KIIFB is funding land acquisition around Kannur Airport as well.

The third one is the Capital City Regional Development Programme. An outer ring road of 78 km through the eastern side of Trivandrum city connecting the Vizhinjam port to the hinder lands is the core of this project. A massive network of Knowledge Hubs, Industrial Parks, Amusement Centres, and Townships on 10,000 acres of land on both sides of the road will be facilitated. The company registered for this purpose will be ready to purchase land in the proposed region at market price from all those willing to sell. The price can be given as land bond or in cash. Those unwilling to sell their land can become shareholders in the Land Pooling Scheme.

## THE CENTRAL GOVERNMENT AND THE GREAT KIIFB CONTROVERSY

The KIIFB was too good to be true. It is not an exaggeration to say that even people sympathetic to the idea were sceptical about its success. But KIIFB was reorganised as per the new Act within three months of the budget announcement and soon overcame its teething problems. The big question was whether KIIFB would be able to mobilise sufficient resources within the expected time frame. To prove the point and announce the arrival in the market, KIIFB successfully placed Masala Bonds through the London Stock Exchange, an achievement that only a few other governmental entities could claim. The opposition raised certain misinformed criticisms. One of the leaders of BJP professional groups filed a legal challenge in the High Court regarding the constitutional validity of a state government entity borrowing from outside the country.

*Controversies Related to CAG*

Public controversy erupted with the Comptroller and Auditing General (CAG) seeking to be appointed in effect as the statutory auditor of the KIIFB. The KIIFB being a commercial organisation under an Act of the assembly, had a clearly laid out procedure to appoint its own statutory auditor. The KIIFB is decidedly under the ambit of the C&AG audit under the provisions in C&AG DPC Act. The C&AG could carry out the audit following the same procedure as in the case of other Public Sector Units (PSUs), and this has been the practice in the KIIFB since its inception. As per the provisions in the Act, the C&AG can audit all the receipts and expenditures of the institutions getting a fixed annual grant from the consolidated fund. It is to be emphasised that this is not limited to the extent of grant given from the consolidated Fund, but all the receipts and expenditure of the institution. C&AG has carried out an audit in the KIIFB as per this provision after the revamp of the organisation.

What C&AG had sought was an audit under a different clause which was not applicable to the KIIFB. The government and the KIIFB made it clear that the KIIFB is open to C&AG audit, but under the normal clause applicable to PSUs. Communications between the government, the C&AG, and the KIIFB were somehow leaked, and the stand taken by the government was misinterpreted as denying a C&AG audit. The opposition began to insinuate that corruption was taking place.

The C&AG's report for the year 2019–20 (State Finance Audit Report) included three pages that questioned the constitutional validity of KIIFB operations. The report alleged that KIIFB's borrowings were off-budget borrowings. They constituted a direct liability of the government. Therefore, KIIFB violated the FRBM Act by borrowing more than what has been mandated by the FRBM Act. Another imputation was that KIIFB borrowing through the Masala bond constituted a violation of clause 293(1), which excludes state governments from borrowing abroad. KIIFB has been equated with the state government and made its borrowings conditional upon FRBM regulations and Art.293(1).

These issues included in the audit report have never been discussed with the state government. Its own rules of procedure stipulate that its reports should not include any point not formally raised with the government, and at any rate, no new point can be included after the discussion of the draft report. Presuming the AG's document to be the draft report, the finance minister publicly repudiated the findings of the AG. This extreme step was taken given the apparent mischief in the report and rumours of the legal challenge to KIIFB coming up in the court.

*The Alleged Breach of Privilege*

The opposition lost no time in slapping a privilege motion against the minister. The final audit report of the AG had to be placed in the State Assembly through the Governor, but the minister publicly disclosed it, and it was an infringement of the privilege of the house, went on the arguments. The reference to the Privileges Committee allowed the government to place its stand in detail.[1] KIIFB is a body corporate created by the legislature and not a part of the state government to which constitutional restrictions on foreign borrowing or restrictions of the FRBM Act apply. Its borrowings were not off-budget because the project expenditure was not a part of government accounts. Off budget borrowing, a common practice by the central government, occurs

[1] The entire discussion of this chapter is based upon the reply given by Finance Minister (2020) to the notice of breach of privilege

when a budget expenditure proposal is partly or wholly met by borrowing by public sector units or such entities and repaid by the government over time.

Most state governments in India have financial institutions like the KIIFB, though not on the same scale, and the C&AG never previously objected to them. KIIFB's borrowings were contingent liabilities and not direct liabilities of the state government. As we have already elaborated earlier, they would become the burden of the state government only in case the asset-liability matching model of the KIIFB fails.

As per the regulations issued by the Reserve Bank of India (RBI), any corporate body was entitled to issue Masala bonds following due procedures with the permission of the Reserve Bank. The argument that the KIIFB Masala Bond defeats 'the purpose and intent of Entry 37 in List 1' of the constitution was silly. The entries in list 1 refer to legislative domains of the central government. The Union parliament, which invoked the legislative powers from this entry, enacted Foreign Exchange Management Act (FEMA), and this Act empowers RBI to regulate foreign loans. As per the guideline issued by RBI, any corporate body can issue Masala bonds after following the prescribed procedure. KIIFB issued masala bonds with the necessary permissions from RBI. So, it was argued that the KIIFB borrowed having fully complied with the rules and regulations and the framework laid down by the Act, the Union Government, and the RBI for foreign borrowing.

The Privileges Committee Report was taken up in the State Assembly for a thorough discussion. A resolution was introduced rejecting the audit paragraphs of the AG regarding the KIIFB. Usually, the report would have been discussed in the Public Accounts Committee (PAC) and placed in the Assembly. But the Privileges Committee in the Assembly had raised the issue, and such a resolution was deemed in order. This ended the attempted *coup d'état* through the agency of the CAG.

*Enforcement Directorate*

The next agency to enter the arena was the Enforcement Directorate (ED), specialising in money laundering. No stretch of imagination can impute that an institution like the KIIFB that mobilises resources from public finance institutions or through bonds whose customers must fully comply with KYC norms could be accused of money laundering. The officers of the KIIFB were asked to travel to Kochi under Covid conditions and were repeatedly made to wait for hours for interrogation. The government was forced to condemn the ED's high-handed measures publicly. It was evident that the ED could not make any headway.

*Income Tax Department*

It was then that the Income Tax Department entered the fray. Their charge was that the KIIFB had paid the contractors without deducting the income tax at the source. The KIIFB's explanation was simple. It had no direct contract with any contractor. SPVs engaged the contractors through open bids. The KIIFB only passed on the payment to the contractors as a service to the SPVs. Concerned SPVs generate and approve the bill. The amount to be deducted as income tax at source and the net payment to the contractor and so on are arrived at by the concerned SPV. The KIIFB simply transfers the tax component to the concerned SPV and the net payment directly to the contractor/ supplier. If any SPV did not remit the tax, it was up to the tax department to take it up with the concerned SPV.

The Income Tax Department initiated an unusual action. A large team of central officials led by the Commissioner himself raided the KIFFB office for a full day and late into the night with live coverage from visual media. The KIIFB had offered to place the password of the computer system with the income tax officials. All transactions of the KIIFB were online, and therefore they could search and read any document at their leisure. They intended to 'raid' KIIFB. No person less than the Union Finance

Minister had attacked the KIIFB in one of the election campaign meetings in Kerala. The quixotic actions by the central agencies were understandable.

Obviously, the inquisition was motivated by the needs of the election. The inaugurations of the completed the KIIFB projects created favourable ripples among the people. The whole exercise was an attempt to tarnish the good image of the institution. One does not know if someone was under the illusion that the raids and the controversies would alienate the investors and damage the KIIFB's performance. They could have also been on a fishing expedition, thinking they would stumble upon some irregularity or malpractice. The KIIFB came through these days of trial by fire with flying colours.

The biggest anti-recession package being implemented in the country is in Kerala. This will support the state economy during the crisis period. It will ensure that infrastructure facilities, which generally require 20 to 25 years from budget allocation, will be materialised in Kerala within the next three years. The benefits will start accruing from now itself rather than decades later. We will also be preventing massive cost escalation if these projects are implemented a few years later. The challenge before Kerala is completing these projects in a time-bound manner and with assured quality.

Chapter 9

# Transforming Kerala's Economic Base from the Present Low Productivity Regime to a High Productivity Knowledge-Economy

The infrastructure development program that we discussed in the last chapter will provide the launchpad for overhauling the technological basis of Kerala's production and services sectors so that the economy is transformed from its current low productivity regime to a high productivity regime that will provide rapid expansion of remunerative and skilled jobs for its educated young labour force. This transition has become imperative given the high and persistent unemployment in the state and declining opportunities for external migration.[1]

The state budget for 2021–22 proposed a comprehensive program for transition to what has been described as the knowledge economy. It is a strategy to increase the knowledge intensity of production and services by focusing on knowledge-intensive sectors and modern technology and innovation. It has four broad components:

1) Technological upgradation of the existing agriculture, agro-based industries, and other micro, small and medium industries, and creating knowledge-intensive operations through knowledge co-creation at the local level.

2) Attracting investment into knowledge industries such as information technology, biotechnology, and promotion of start-ups. Besides knowledge-intensive industries, service-based industries such as tourism and skill-based industries

[1] The discussion in this chapter is based on Thomas Isaac (2021), Balagopal (2021) and K-DISC (2021).

such as light engineering and hardware are also prioritised.

3) Taking advantage of the global employment trend towards the gig economy by a massive program of digital skilling of the unemployed and the educated who are out of the labour force.

4) Restructuring higher education to promote knowledge production and innovation and better integration with knowledge application programmes locally and globally.

In the present chapter, we shall briefly discuss the above action points.

## MODERNISING THE TRADITIONAL SECTORS

The first component is integrating science and technology into the different livelihood sectors so that these activities can become more remunerative and market competitive. Agricultural productivity will have to be increased sustainably, and the output converted into value-added products. By moving up the value chain, the agri-entrepreneurs can improve the producers' share in the product's final value.

Let us, for instance, examine the case of coconut cultivation, the most important crop of the state (Isaac and Mathai, 2021). Coconut cultivation practices have not improved; the labour-intensive cultural practices and inter-crop cultivation have disappeared. The net result is that the productivity of coconut cultivation in Kerala is currently less than half of that in Tamil Nadu. The technology of processing coconut husks into coir and coir products has stagnated for the last two centuries, so Kerala's monopoly in coir production has shrunk to 10–20 per cent of the national output. Similarly, coconut oil production has now shifted out of the state. There is hardly any value addition in coconut output in the state.

The most important reason for the disappearance of some cultural practices, like periodic cleaning of the crown of the coconut and regular plucking of the coconut, is the dearth of coconut climbers. To date, Kerala has failed to invent a motorised climber. The bane of coconut cultivators has been the steady expansion of root wilt disease from central Kerala covering more than half the cultivated area. No solution for this problem has been identified so far. The proposal is now to cut the diseased palms and replant them with saplings from elite trees. The alternative of developing the tissue culture has not been pursued in earnest.

The eclipse of the coir industry in Kerala results from the dependence on handicraft technology. Mechanisation is currently promoted. But it is not going to be an issue of mechanisation alone. We must explore the possibilities of diversification of products such as composites. Of promise is the binder-less board manufactured by exerting high pressure on coconut husk powder or waste under high temperature, whereby the lignin in the husk would melt and act as a natural binder. It would be a perfect wood substitute with no chemicals and better properties than regular composites and plywood. This innovation is still in the prototype stage, and its eventual deployment can alone result in a value addition of Rs 1500 crores. Similarly, Kerala has to ensure that its coconut oil extraction and other value-added products are nationally competitive.

If the coffee growers of Wayanad, who have been in the throes of crisis for the last three decades, modify their cultural practices and manufacture their own brand of coffee powder, their incomes can be substantially improved. If they take a step further to reduce the carbon emission and plant sufficient trees for sequestrating the net emission converting the district into carbon-neutral, it will significantly facilitate the branding of the coffee. It would also have spin-offs such as additional income from eco-tourism, processing of fruits, carbon credit, and tree mortgage banking.

The traditional industries of Kerala also would have to be restructured from handicrafts to modern technology. As we noted in chapter 5, it is the Micro, Small and Medium Enterprises (MSME) sector rather than the factory sector growing in Kerala. The budget has also proposed promoting industrial clusters sponsored by the local governments to generate five non-agricultural employments for every 1000 population. If small sector-based growth must be dynamic, it must be innovation-led and continuously technology upgraded.

## INVESTMENT IN KNOWLEDGE – SKILL – SERVICE INTENSIVE INDUSTRIES

Private investment in Kerala has been poor. We have argued that the so-called labour militancy and radical politics being a barrier to private investment is primarily an ideological construct created by the anti-communist movements of the late 1950s and early 1960s. The initial phase of the trade union movement was indeed confronted with violent containment strategies by the firms, which led to militant tactics. But as the trade union movement stabilised and collective bargaining systems became widespread, the strikes and lockouts declined. Regarding the incidence of labour disputes or days of employment lost, Kerala has been much below the national average since the 1970s. The share of wages and emoluments in the value-added in the factory sector has been consistently lower in the state. Nevertheless, the image of Kerala being an anti-investor has been deliberately propagated whenever the Left comes to power.

The state has been held back for want of infrastructure development and from its low rank in ease of doing business. Kerala cannot waive labour rights or environmental regulations; that is not an option for the Left Democratic Front government. Nevertheless, the state has set the target of moving up in the top 10 bracket in the national Ease of Doing Business Ranking. The period 2016–21 witnessed a large number of green shoots emerging, and the budget speeches have listed the major investments in the pipeline or that are being implemented. A big challenge would be to make Kerala an attractive investment destination. Pharmaceuticals, genome sequencing, medical devices, electronic hardware, light engineering, tourism, rubber products, Information Technology (IT), and Information Technology Enabled Services (ITES) have been identified as sectors of particular importance. However, the Covid interruption broke the momentum, and the final realised investment fell much below expectations.

Meanwhile, the public sector units in Kerala have been revamped and, on the whole, are working at a profit. The state has also been staking claim to takeover central PSUs facing privatisation. Our experience is that the price of land alone more than pays for their rehabilitation. The efficient and successful functioning of the state PSUs would be a major argument in support of a favourable investment climate in Kerala.

Historically the entrepreneurial classes of Kerala have been relatively weak, and it was an important reason for the lack of industrial dynamism. However, the success of start-up enterprises opens a possibility of a new generation of professional youth on the strength of their innovations filling up the gap in entrepreneurial talents. During 2016–21, the number of start-ups in Kerala increased from 300 to 3900, employing 32,000 persons. A comprehensive package, which includes technology innovation zones, incubation centres, accelerators, special finance schemes including venture capital fund, and working capital accommodation, up to 90 per cent of the work order has been announced.

Continuous innovation is necessary for any successful start-up program and upgradation of the different economic sectors. A four-point action plan for promoting innovations and creating a conducive environment has been chalked out:

1. The first is a 3-tier comprehensive Kerala Innovation Challenge, with attractive monetary incentives involving all higher education institutions. At the district level, 8000 participants would be given a prize of Rs 25,000. The shortlisted

2000 would participate at the state level and be given a prize of Rs 50,000. Those innovations selected at the state level would be supported for three years to convert their prototypes into products.

2. Local practical experience could also be tapped for identifying innovations. Any person who has ideas and techniques to solve practical problems in their locality can upload their ideas on a digital platform, where they would be evaluated with the help of experts; selected innovations will be given mentoring and financial assistance to develop them into products. Alternatively, the problems in different development sectors may be listed, and the collaboration of experts in universities and other institutions sought to solve them. Promoting local innovation through the local innovation programmes around day-to-day life and livelihood would emerge as a major bottom-up innovation strategy within this framework.

3. The local governments in Kerala implement projects rather than schemes. Therefore, the possibilities of local-level innovations are very high. Some such innovations in the past, such as the beneficiary-managed local drinking water project, have been scaled up to the national level by the World Bank. Local governments innovated on some of these state-level schemes, such as Buds Schools for the differently-abled children, family-level micro-planning for poverty eradication, crime mapping and so on. A special fund has been earmarked for promoting innovative projects of local governments. Improving the application of innovation in local government for local economic development and better governance at the local government level through One Local Government One Idea (OLOI) programme would be another component for grassroots level innovation application.

4. Strengthening the application of innovation in developing innovation clusters with the exponential growth of MSMEs

would develop as a major component of value creation and local employment generation of the skilled and semi-skilled. Start-up innovation zones will be set up in government departments.

The triple plus helix model with University-Industry, Industry-Government and Government-University interactions has been highlighted as the regional innovation promotion model for the Knowledge Society. Efforts have been made to create this system in Kerala around Kerala Development and Innovation Strategic Council's (K-DISC) innovation programmes. The budget announcement of creating a knowledge economy fund would go a long way in further strengthening these innovation systems. This would further improve the democratisation of innovation, eventually leading to new start-ups and developing Intellectual Property (IP).

The emerging technology programmes have successfully showcased the application of Artificial Intelligence, Block-chain, Internet of Things, Telemetry, Augmented Reality and Virtual Reality in various cases at the state government and the PSU level. These have culminated in a few co-ordinated programmes with International Universities and National Institutions in core areas such as:

1. Safe to eat food for traceability and total supply chain development in agriculture, animal husbandry, fisheries, and dairy, linking the distributed production systems through aggregators to the market with interventions for improving shelf life and minimal processing;
2. Establishing an evidence-based Ayur-tech and wellness industry around systems for herbal-based holistic healthcare using traceability, genomic processing, improved scientific diagnosis, analytics based on scientific experiments, enhanced availability of medicines at affordable cost, standardisation of

practices, better quality systems and wellness tourism;
3. Strengthening electric vehicle and green energy programme around the manufacture of Lithium Titanate and Lithium Iron Phosphate Batteries, Development of Battery Management systems and Power Control Systems and Brushless DC Motors, Permanent Magnet Synchronous Motors and decentralised solar generation and microgrids around concepts of carbon neutrality, climate change, and energy conservation programmes;
4. Strengthening fintech initiatives around mass-based large volume, low-value thrift transactions, working capital for livelihood, small enterprise creation, and maintaining social security in the informal sector;
5. And improving geriatric care systems through active ageing programmes focussing on nutrition management, intervention for cognitive wellness, digital equity programmes, improving social security for the elderly around better participation in economic activities, developing technology system around safe elderly spaces based on a concept of ageing in place and innovative plans for enabling daily activities of living which will enhance independence and dignity of the elderly.

## MISSION FOR HOME/NEAR HOME-BASED DIGITAL EMPLOYMENT

As we have already noted, unemployment of the educated is the biggest developmental challenge faced by Kerala. While the national unemployment level in the age group of 15 to 59 was 5.8 per cent in 2018–19, it was 10.4 per cent in Kerala. While the male unemployment rate in Kerala is 5.8 per cent, the female unemployment rate is 19.1 per cent. Because of the discouraging effect of prolonged unemployment, women stop seeking jobs and exit from the labour force. As a result, while the labour participation rate of men is 73.5 per cent, that of women is only 28.5 per cent.

It is estimated that in Kerala, 5 lakh women professionals have taken a career break and 30 lakh educated women who are outside the labour force would be willing to work from home or near home. Besides, 16 lakh educated youngsters registered with the employment exchange are waiting for employment.

The Covid crisis also provides an opportunity for Kerala. Working from home will be the post-Covid normal in jobs that can be done digitally. The number of such workers was around three crores during the first Covid wave; it is expected to increase to 15–18 crores globally in the next five years. If one is working from home, it does not matter whether the house is in New York or Kochi. If Kerala can attract 2 million jobs from this potential global employment pool, it would dramatically change the state's economic base within a short period.

TO CONNECT THE DEMAND WITH THE SUPPLY INVOLVES THREE MAJOR STEPS.

One, the unemployed, the underemployed, and those who have withdrawn from employment will have to be mobilised, and their aptitude and capabilities assessed. They would have to be divided into different categories, such as those who fully meet the demand requirements, those who would require skilling, those who would need support to acquire primary computer skills, and so on. With the help of local governments and social movements, it would require a campaign to motivate potential workers to register at a Digital Workforce Management System. Their accurate classification in the system would require interaction with the applicants and counselling through appropriate agencies.

Two, considering the demand requirements and aptitude of job seekers, a massive skilling program would have to be initiated, through a coordinated action of existing skilling agencies, higher education and technical institutions, and similar agencies willing to be involved. The existing skilling capacities would have to be enhanced many folds, the pace of skilling accelerated, and its quality raised to international norms. This, in fact, is the biggest challenge.

Third, continuous monitoring of evolving global job markets and aggregating the demand is required. It would involve creating a digital platform for efficient management of supply and demand-side opportunities and matching those opportunities to the skilling program. Those who qualify for this skilling program would be placed on the platform to meet the global demand. In a sense, the government of Kerala agencies would assure the skill quality of the job seekers on the platform. The local knowledge co-creation activities open opportunities for local demand creation of knowledge-intensive jobs making the labour market robust and not wholly dependent on the global economy.

However, there is one warning raised — the danger of the digital divide. It is precisely to avoid this danger that as the first step, we have digitalized schools. The next logical step is to ensure the availability of at least one laptop in every household for which a special scheme has been announced. The K-FON, which we discussed in the last chapter, would provide free internet to all households and institutions and to the poor. The intake of students to higher education would be expanded drastically, and the quality would improve.

The second concern has been from the trade union movement. The gig economy has been criticized for splintering the labour force and undermining unionisation. The Kerala project is not focused on existing production units but on the unemployed and those withdrawn from the labour force. The strategy is also to provide small workstations to work from near home. Finally, there is active intermediation of state government and its agencies; very importantly, the state government guarantees the workers' social security and insurance.

Efforts to create alternatives to the platform economy models of global capital, which had been pushing highly exploitive algorithms, are also significant in this context. Models around the cooperative-based innovation collectives, farmers production organisations and collectives of knowledge workers with guiding principles of decent and fairer returns to the stakeholders on the value of labour and sustainability of the enterprise will be encouraged. These need to be pursued through networking at the international level. The program also includes continuous upgrading of the workers' skills so that there is upward job mobility.

Kerala Government has already set up Kerala Knowledge-Economy Mission (KKEM) which has been made responsible for undertaking the three tasks listed above and linking the digital platform with the social security payments to the workers. The Government has approved a comprehensive strategy paper. Kerala Development and Innovation Strategic Council (KDISC) is the key institution for the overall coordination of the digital employment program with the programs for innovation and restructuring of higher education.

## TOWARDS EXCELLENCE IN HIGHER EDUCATION

The Kerala Universities and departments perform poorly in the prominent global rankings published by the Times Higher Education and the Shanghai Ranking Consultancy. Investment in higher education must be increased manifold. Similarly, the approach to teaching and research needs a paradigm shift. Both are not easy but are essential for the economic transformation we have outlined.

The enrolment ratio in the higher education sector must be raised to at least 75 per cent. The all-India average is 26 per cent. It will be around 50 per cent in Kerala if the Kerala students in other states are also included. It would imply an expansion of education facilities and faculty strength in the universities and affiliated colleges. There is also the suggestion to introduce a shift system in selected high-performing colleges. As in the case of schools,

KIIFB funds would be used to upgrade the infrastructure facilities in the universities, digitalize the college classrooms, and improve the infrastructure in the government colleges.

A radical proposal has been to set up 30 fully autonomous centres of excellence within the universities so that the existing system does not encumber them. The directors of these schools would be appointed through special search committees from national and international levels and would be given maximum freedom in setting up the institutions. Based on objective criteria and growth potential, some existing departments may be converted into excellence centres. This is a major departure from the existing practice where such centres are set up outside the university system like the Centre for Development Studies, Centre for Earth Science Studies, Sri Chitra Tirunal Centre, etc., with high national repute. However, their linkage impact on the university system where the bulk of the students study has been minimal.

It is at the post-doctoral level that contributes to knowledge production mainly takes place. The number of doctoral students will be expanded, and 500 post-doctoral fellowships ranging from Rs . 50000 to Rs . 100000 per month will be instituted. There would be additional support for laboratory facilities. The post-doctoral fellowships will be open to all scholars in India and abroad. These fellowships will be linked to key developmental challenges in the economy. The universities, Higher Education Council and education experts are drawing up a comprehensive scheme for a rapid upgradation of the university system. The post-doctoral programme could also be linked to the coordinated projects for knowledge co-creation programme for linking the real-life problem of the local economy with solutions from the university system elsewhere, thus creating vibrant local knowledge application and knowledge development space focusing on IP creation, value addition and productivity enhancement.

We have briefly surveyed the broad contours of the knowledge economy that Kerala aspires. It would imply a vibrant higher education system that would create knowledge and absorb knowledge from outside, an environment that constantly innovates them into new products and processes and integrates innovations into the production of goods and services. It also includes a strategy to attract digital employment from recent trends in global employment through a digital platform that would aggregate the demand and supply of job seekers skilled through a massive skilling program. The sharp reduction in educated unemployment, acceleration in economic growth and improvement in environmental standards would be the outcomes of such a strategy.

Chapter 10

# Conclusion: Looking Forward

The 2021 May elections to the Assembly turned out to be a historic break with the tradition of the two fronts alternating in the state government. The Left won a resounding victory, increasing vote percentage from 43.35 in 2016 to 45.28 and the number of seats from 91 to 99. Even though almost all the pre-poll surveys predicted a Left victory, the opposition ran a virulent campaign against the government. Their hope sprang from the Parliament Election 2019 when they won 19 of the 20 parliament seats. In the 2019 election, their vote share increased from 38.79 in 2016 to 47.23 per cent, and LDF's declined to 35.10 per cent. It was an electoral debacle for the Left (See Table 3.1).

An important reason for the electoral outcome was the polarisation of votes favouring the Congress, which alone was a possible electoral alternative to the BJP at the centre. The Sabarimala temple controversy also adversely affected the Left. The forest temple of Sabarimala is the greatest pilgrimage centre in Kerala, attracting devotees from all over South India. By tradition, entry of women of menstruating age to the temple premises is prohibited. At the end of long-drawn-out litigation, the Supreme Court struck down the rule discriminating against women, and the Left supported the court verdict. Sensing the groundswell of the sentiments of a significant section of the devotees against women's temple entry, the opposition parties, both the Congress and BJP, who had initially welcomed the court verdict, executed a volte-face and started agitation against the government. This influenced a section of the voters, and Congress benefited more than the BJP. There was a sharp decline in the vote share of the Left among all Hindu communities. The database for Table 3.2 also showed that the decline among the minority communities is relatively lower.

## THE 2021 ELECTIONS TO THE ASSEMBLY

In the local government elections in 2020, the LDF staged a comeback, winning 42.53 per cent of votes (See Table 3.1). The UDF vote share declined to 38.64 per cent, and the NDA vote share remained around the same level at 15 per cent. The LDF won 61 per cent of the Grama Panchayats, 73 per cent of the Block Panchayats, and 86 per cent of the District Panchayats. In the urban areas, the LDF won 50 per cent of the Municipalities, and all but 1 of the 6 Corporations. The opposition tried to resurrect the Sabarimala issue in the 2021 election; the Left refused to bite it and stuck to its discourse on development achievements and successful covid strategy. The pre-poll surveys revealed that there was no anti-incumbency, and the majority of the population, including a section of UDF voters, agreed on Pinarayi Vijayan to be their choice for the Chief Ministership. Thus, the jinx was broken.

The CSDS Survey for 2021 (same source as for Table 3.2) found that 53 per cent of the poor voted for the LDF, against 30 per cent for the UDF, and 15 per cent for the NDA. This should not surprise anyone. The poor have always been the vote base of the Left, and its share tends to decline as one moves up the income categories. However, it is surprising that the Left received 41 per cent of the votes of the middle and richer classes. There has been a shift in the middle and upper strata favouring the Left, making up for the loss to the BJP of some of the poor. The support of the LDF was relatively higher among youth and women.

The LDF vote share among the Christian and Muslim minorities increased from a historic 30 per cent to 39 per cent. The

Left's consistent defence of secularism and the fading of illusions regarding Congress during the parliament election resulted in a shift favouring the Left. Further, the Left has made an effort to appreciate the nature of the religiosity among the Christians and the Muslims and reach out to their concerns.

Although the BJP made serious efforts to increase its influence among the minorities, it is still negligible. But they have shed their upper-caste image to an extent and increased their support among the backward castes and even Dalits. However, the indication is that their expansion has plateaued off. The NDA vote share had stagnated around 15 per cent in the 2016 state assembly and local government elections. In the 2021 assembly election, despite their heavily funded campaign, their vote share declined to 12.49 per cent. They lost the lone seat they had held in the state assembly.

The election results of 2021 do not prove that the Left overcame its handicaps in capturing a stable majority above 50 per cent in Kerala. In fact, its vote share is still below the historic high of 48.63 per cent vote share achieved in 2006, despite the entry of two minor political parties from the UDF to the LDF. However, the election victory of 2021 has laid the ground for a much broader shift in popular support. The prospects of being out of power continuously for two terms for the first time have demoralized the UDF, and a dropout process is very evident. But the BJP has lost lustre, and the LDF has become an attractive option for them. The support from minority communities has increased, and bridges are being built with the middle classes.

In short, we can expect a new phase of expansion of the popular base for the Left in Kerala and a prospect of yet another electoral victory in 2026. It provides a rare opportunity for continuity in policy and a chance to complete the agenda discussed in the last two chapters.

THE NEW AGENDA

The agenda has been set out in detail in the 900 points programs in the Election Manifesto of LDF. The plan may be summed up in three broad steps – a hop, step, and jump strategy — to add a little bit of humour.

The first is the welfare and social security of ordinary people. We have already discussed, at length, the historical evolution of the redistributive strategy of development which ensured a much higher quality of life and welfare to the people in the state (Chapter 4). In this respect, 2016–21 government's stellar achievements were an important factor in the election victory (Chapter 7).

In the SDG achievement ranking, Kerala tops India with a score of 75. In the world ranking, India's position is way below, at 117, while Kerala's score would rank it around 73. The state is poised to reach the SDG goals by 2030 in most sectors, particularly health, education, hunger, and poverty. Kerala can now aim to eradicate absolute poverty by providing every family with housing, electricity, drinking water, sanitation, minimum food, educational services, and health care. Livelihood occupations would be protected and expanded.

Democratic decentralisation (Chapter 6) will continue to be the strategy to achieve the SDG goals. The PPC's achievements have been remarkable, but our discussion also identified several weaknesses that must be overcome. The twenty-fifth anniversary of the PPC will be an appropriate moment to launch a renewed drive to make democratic decentralization more participatory, transparent, and effective.

The second step is overcoming the infrastructure deficit in the state. We have discussed at fair length the major infrastructure investment program led by the KIIFB and launched by the 2016–2021 government (Chapter 8). All these projects will be completed during 2021–26. As we noted, other major infrastructure programs like industrial corridors are also envisaged. A common feature of these programs is being primarily financed outside the budget. Their implementation would remove a major handicap impeding investment and growth.

The next challenge is how to leverage the new infrastructure to transform Kerala's economic base. This final leap has been the main theme of the budget for 2021–22 (Chapter 9). Thus, for example, the KIIFB finances the K-FON project to provide assured broadband internet connectivity to all institutions and households and electricity projects to overhaul the transmission and distribution lines. Their completion will create pre-conditions for Kerala to reap employment opportunities for working from home in the digital world. Upon completion of the industrial parks, private investment can be attracted into sectors where we have greater competitive advantages. The KIIFB investment in higher education can convert it into the basis for the production of knowledge and innovation, which will invigorate the traditional sectors or promote start-ups. All these inter-related activities are being captured in the phrase *knowledge economy*. It implies rapidly modernizing its economic base into a high productivity knowledge-skill-service-based economy, which will generate quality jobs for educated unemployed youth.

## ENVIRONMENT, GENDER, SOCIAL JUSTICE AND PROGRESSIVE CULTURE

The objective of the development strategy outlined above is not the neoliberal imperative of 'maximize growth at any cost.' Rather, the aim is to *optimize growth* within redistribution, environmental sustainability, gender and social justice, and concerns of progressive culture. Only such a perspective can be a genuine alternative to the neoliberal growth strategy.

*Environment*

One important reason for the knowledge economy orientation has been that it would be more appropriate to the state's endowments of natural and human resources. Kerala's development process has resulted in resource depletion, deforestation, reclamation of the wetlands, pollution of water bodies and atmosphere, and unsanitary conditions. In the era of climate change, the state is forced to pay a heavy price owing to natural disasters and pandemics (Chapter 7).

A powerful environment movement and growing widespread awareness of environmental issues have been a positive trend. What is attempted is a two-pronged approach. The first is the macro regulatory framework for land use, pollution control, coastal regulation, protection of environmentally fragile areas, afforestation, and so on. The second is local level disaster management and disaster mitigation programs of the local governments. We have referred to watershed planning, sanitation, tree planting program, carbon-neutral drives, and local disaster action plans.

*Gender*

Despite the better condition of women in Kerala, the gender reality has been one of discrimination, violence, and lower social status. Recently there has been explicit integration of gender concerns through gender budgeting at the local and state levels, through the promotion of women agencies such as Kudumbasree, and attempts to strengthen women protection measures. It is hoped that large-scale integration of unemployed and out-of-employment women into the labour force in the knowledge economy and focus on modernization of livelihood would contribute to the reversal of women's marginalisation in the development process. The crime mapping of violence against women and preventive measures as part of the local government's Women Component Plan is a program with much potential.

*Social Justice*

We have discussed the success of Kerala in poverty alleviation through multi-sectoral interventions. Now the declared objective is to eradicate absolute poverty through micro-planning. At the same time, it is crucial to bear in mind that there are historically socio-economically marginalized caste and communities for whom special focus and consideration would be provided in the development strategy.

In Chapter 2, we pointed out how the coup d'état against the 1957 Communist ministry delayed the implementation of land reform by more than a decade. This delay resulted in the disappearance of surplus land and denying the agricultural workers their right to cultivable land. The neoliberal privatization program is now foreclosing their job opportunities in the public sector. The implementation of SCP and TSP must be improved and made genuinely participatory. The focus on best education to improve social mobility, social placement in jobs and promotion of entrepreneurship holds the key.

*Progressive Culture*

Investment in culture is vital to preserving Kerala's progressive and secular cultural traditions. As the per capita income rises, the deployment of this purchasing power will be an important question. Today it is promoting a wasteful consumerist culture — consumption for its own sake. Keralites purchased more gold and consumer durables and constructed costly and tasteless houses. Such a consumer culture is against all socialist ideals.

So, what are the alternative avenues for expenditure? People should consume more cultural goods and services. But to do that, more cultural infrastructure is required. An appropriate mindset must be created to make that possible. A rapidly developing economy like Kerala must invest in history and culture; otherwise, not socialist ideals but ideals of consumerism will dominate. There has been criticism for spending borrowed funds on cultural infrastructures. Promotion of culture and heritage is good in itself, but it also could have interesting spin-offs in tourism and education.

Leftist ethos and cultural hegemony are under threat. Hindu society in Kerala underwent a renaissance from the late nineteenth century. It had become the most secular society, but that is being challenged now. There is a need to acknowledge and confront the threat. Part of the solution is to go back to our heritage and authentic history; show how cosmopolitan and accommodative it was.

## PROSPECTS FOR THE FUTURE

The new government's successful implementation of the above agenda can trigger significant political ramifications inside Kerala and across India. Within Kerala, it would strengthen the traditional class-based movements in agriculture and industries by improving productivity and better returns to the stakeholders. The program of infrastructure construction, generation of quality employment, and restructuring of higher education would appeal to the younger generation and the growing middle class. It also has the potential of mobilizing the intellectual and skill capabilities of the Malayalee diaspora in transforming Kerala into a knowledge economy. In short, the agenda can provide the basis for a broad-based coalition of basic classes who have traditionally supported the LDF and the new middle class in Kerala.

Such an alternative model would provide a source of inspiration for alternative policies. In the opening chapter of this monograph, after describing the challenges of neoliberal globalization, we had promised to lay bare the process of Kerala's engagement with the neoliberal federal system. Within the ever-tightening restrictions imposed by the Union government, Kerala has pursued alternative policies of protecting the public sector, health, and education with highly positive outcomes. These outcomes, in turn, have strengthened the social security and care systems and drastically reduced hunger and poverty. Democratic decentralization has provided the framework for implementing such a program with the participation of the people.

It is a tragedy that most states in India, in a fit of neoliberal fervour, have chosen not to spend even the surplus financial resources to provide people's basic needs lest they incur a revenue deficit in contravention to the FRBM Act. On the eve of Covid, all states in India together had a treasury surplus of Rs 1.5 lakh crores that they had deposited in the government of India securities at a much lower rate of interest than the interest they paid for public borrowing. As per the statement of the Union Finance Minister in the parliament is, deposits had ballooned to Rs 3 lakh crores by the end of November 2021 (Isaac, 2021). Most states are now not taking the permissible public borrowing of 3 per cent of GSDP to minimise such negative interest arbitrage. The fiscal deficit of states in 2019–20 was only 2.49 (see Table 5.3). The Kerala experience would promote political pressure to reject absurd neoliberal cretinism.

This is not a call for replicating Kerala in other places. It is to drive home this point that we have devoted two chapters to document Kerala's political evolution that fashioned the redistributive strategy (chapters 2 and 3) and yet another chapter on the specifics of working out of the redistributive strategy (chapter 4). The experience of other southern states like Tamil Nadu is also relevant in this context. Kerala calls for a proactive state in favour of the welfare of the people.

The current strategy of infrastructure construction and the transformation of the economic base into a knowledge economy rebuts the hesitation regarding the backwash effect of redistribution undermining growth. Growth with equity is possible and feasible.

Today Kerala presents a picture of high social achievements on a weak economic base and an unacceptable level of unemployment. The case of Gujarat may be a picture in contrast — a rapidly industrializing and growing state but very poor social attainments and deprivation for the poor. Of course, the central and north Indian states have neither growth nor equity. Kerala is on a course to create an economy that ensures high growth and high equity. This has come to be called the Nava Kerala or New Kerala Model.

## References

Agarwal, Bina (2017): 'Does group farming empower rural women? The Indian experience', Discussion paper. UN Women, New York

Baiocchi, Gianpaolo (1999): 'Participation, Activism, and Politics: The Porto Alegre Experiment and Deliberative Democratic Theory'. Paper presented at the Real Utopias Project Conference V: Experiments in Empowered Deliberative Democracy, 14–16 January 2000. University of Wisconsin, Madison

Balagopal K.N. (2021): *Revised Budget Speech 2021–22*, Government of Kerala, Thiruvananthapuram

Baru R. (1999): 'Missionaries in Medical Care', *Economic and Political Weekly*, Vol. 34, Issue No. 9

Centre for Development Studies (1975): *Poverty, Unemployment and Development Policy: A Case Study of Selected Issues with Special Reference to Kerala*. United Nations Department of Economic and Social Affairs, New York

Central Water Commission (2018): *Study Report Kerala Floods of August 2018*

Chakraborty, Achin (2005): 'Kerala's Changing Development Narratives', *Economic and Political Weekly*, Vol. 40, Issue No. 6

Communist Party of India (Marxist) (2018): *Keralathile Communist Partyude Charithram, Bhagam –1, 1940 vare*, (History of Communist Party in Kerala Part –1, up to 1940). Chintha Publishers, Thiruvananthapuram

——— (2019): *Keralathile Communist Partyude Charithram, Bhagam – 2, 1940–1952* (History of Communist Party in Kerala Part – 2, 1940–1952). Chintha Publishers, Thiruvananthapuram

——— (2020): *Keralathile Communist Partyude Charithram,*

*Bhagam – 3, 1953–1964* (History of Communist Party in Kerala Part – 3, 1953–1964). Chintha Publishers, Thiruvananthapuram

Ekbal, B. (2006): *Kerala — Aarogya Mathruka: Vijayathil Ninnum Prathisandhiyilekku* (Kerala Model of Health: From Success to Crisis). Mathrubhumi Books, Kozhikode

——— (2019): 'Kerala Model of Health: From Success to Crisis', in *Restructuring, Kerala Economy, Problems, Policies and Perspectives*, edited by Abdul Salim. Orient Blackswan, Hyderabad

Franke, Richard W. (1996): *Life is a Little Better: Redistribution as a Development Strategy in Nadur Village, Kerala*, 2nd ed. Promila & Company, New Delhi. (First published in 1993)

——— and Barbara H., Chasin (1994): *Kerala: Radical Reform as Development in an Indian State*, 2nd ed. Institute for Food and Development Policy. California, Oakland

Fung, Archon, and Erik Olin Wright. (2003): 'Thinking about Empowered Participatory Governance', *Deepening Democracy: Institutional Innovations in Empowered Participatory Governance*, Archon Fung and Erik Olin Wright, eds. The Real Utopias Project IV, Pages 3–42. Verso: London and New York

Ganuza, Ernesto and Gianpaolo Baiocchi. (2012): 'The Power of Ambiguity: How Participatory Budgeting Travels the Globe', 8 (2) *Journal of Public Deliberation*, http://www.publicdeliberation.net/jpd/vol8/iss2/art8

George, K. K. (1993): Limits to Kerala Model of Development: An Analysis of Fiscal Crisis and Its Implications, Centre for Development Studies Monograph Series, Thiruvananthapuram

——— and Ajith N. Kumar (1999): 'What Is Wrong with Kerala's Education System?', Working Paper No. 3, Centre for Socio-economic and Environment Studies (CSES), Kochi

Gopakumar, G. (2004): Lokniti Survey, CSDS, https://www.sciencespo.fr/ceri/sites/sciencespo.fr.ceri/files/elections.pdf

Gulati, I.S. and Modi, Ashok (1983): 'Remittances of Indian Migrants to the Middle East: An Assessment with Special

Reference to Migrants from Kerala', Working Paper No. 182, Centre for Development Studies

Harnecker, Marta (2015): *A World to Build: New Paths Toward Twenty-First Century Socialism.* Monthly Review Press, New York

——— and Bartolome, Jose (2019): *Planning from Below: A Decentralized Participatory Planning Proposal,* with the collaboration of Noel López and translated by Federico Fuentes. Monthly Review Press, New York

*The Hindu* (2021): https://www.thehindu.com/elections/kerala-assembly/christians-muslims-dalits-and-obcs-backed-ldf-says-csds-lokniti-survey/article34502148.ece?homepage=true

The Hindu Data Team (2021): 'Excess deaths' during the pandemic in India, The Hindu, 11 September 2021, Chennai

*The Indian Express* (2021): https://www.newindianexpress.com/states/kerala/2021/mar/20/massive-shift-of-nair-ezhava-vote-base-fuels-saffron-surge-in-kerala-2278945.html

Jose, A.V. (2021): 'The story of social spending – A revisit to the Kerala model of development – Part II' in Kerala Economy, Volume 2 No. 1, January, Gulati Institute of Finance and Taxation, Thiruvananthapuram

Kabir, M. and Krishnan, T.N. (1991): 'Social Intermediation and Health Transition: Lessons from Kerala', Thiruvananthapuram: Centre for Development Studies Working Paper 251

Kannan, K.P. (2005): 'Kerala's Turnaround in Growth: Role of Social Development, Remittances and Reform', *Economic and Political Weekly*, Vol. 40 Issue No. 6

——— (2016): 'Housing Condition in Kerala with special focus on Rural areas and Socially Disadvantaged Sections', Volume I, Main Report, Laurie Baker Centre for Habitat Studies, Thiruvananthapuram

———, K.R. Thankappan, V. Ramankutty, and K. P. Aravindan. (1991): 'Health and Development in Rural Kerala: A Study of the Linkages Between Socio-Economic Status and Health

Status'. IRTC and KSSP, Pallakad

———, Khan, Imran (2016): 'Housing Condition in Kerala with special focus on Rural areas and Socially Disadvantaged Sections, Laurie Baker Centre for Habitat Studies Vilappilsala', Trivandrum, Volume I, Main Report

———, Hari, K. S. (2020): 'Revisiting Kerala's Gulf Connection: Half a Century of Emigration, Remittances and Their Macroeconomic Impact, 1972–2020', *The Indian Journal of Labour Economics*, 63(4)

K-DISC (2021): 'Strategy Paper — Comprehensive Programme for Employment of the Educated Unemployed in Kerala', Kerala Knowledge Economy Mission, Vol I, II, III, Thiruvananthapuram

Kerala State Planning Board (1988): *Economic Review 1987*, Thiruvananthapuram

——— (1990): *Economic Review 1989*, Thiruvananthapuram

——— (2017): *Economic Review 2016*, Thiruvananthapuram

——— (2019): *Economic Review 2018*, Thiruvananthapuram

——— (2019): *A Special Package for Post-Flood Kuttanad*, Thiruvananthapuram

——— (2020): *Economic Review 2019*, Thiruvananthapuram

Kingdom, Geeta Gandhi (2007): 'The Progress of School Education in India', *Oxford Review of Economic Policy*, Vol. 23, Issue No. 2

Krishnan, T.N. (1991): 'Wages, Employment and Output in Interrelated Labour Markets in an Agrarian Economy — A Study of Kerala', *Economic and Political Weekly*, Vol. 26, Issue No. 26

Lieten, G. K. (1982): *The First Communist Ministry in Kerala, 1957–59*. K. P. Bagchi & Company, Calcutta

Mencher, Joan (1980): 'The Lessons and Non-Lessons of Kerala', *Economic and Political Weekly* Vol. 15, Issue No. 41– 42– 43

Mukherjee, C. and Thomas Isaac, T.M, (1994): 'Nine Observations on Educated Unemployment in Kerala', in International Congress on Kerala Studies – Abstracts, Vol. 2, AKG Centre for Research and Studies, Thiruvananthapuram

Namboothirpad, EMS (1948): *Keralam Malayalikalude Mathrubhumi.* Chintha Publishers (Reprint), Thiruvananthapuram

——— (1978): 'Note on Report of the Committee on Panchayat Raj Institutions', In Report of the Committee on Panchayat Raj Institutions, Government of India, New Delhi

——— (1984): *Kerala Society and Politics: A Historical Survey.* National Book Centre, New Delhi

——— (1986): *Communist Party Keralathil: Bhagam I.* Chintha Publishers, Thiruvananthapuram

——— (1986): *Communist Party Keralathil: Bhagam II.* Chintha Publishers, Thiruvananthapuram

——— (1987): *Communist Party Keralathil: Bhagam III.* Chintha Publishers, Thiruvananthapuram

——— (1994): *Communist Party in Kerala: Six Decades of Struggle and Advance.* National Book Centre, New Delhi

——— (1994) Presidential Address, International Congress on Kerala Studies. A.K.G. Centre for Research and Studies, Thiruvananthapuram

Narayana, D. (1990): 'Agricultural economy of Kerala in the post-seventies: stagnation of cycles?', Working Paper 235, Centre for Development Studies, Thiruvananthapuram

National Sample Survey Office (2015): 'Key indicators of Social Consumption in India: Health, NSS 71st round, January – June 2014', Ministry of Statistics and Programme Implementation, Government of India, New Delhi

——— (2018): 'Key Indicators of Social Consumption in India: Health, NSS 75th round, July 2017 – June 2018', Ministry of Statistics and Programme Implementation, Government of India, New Delhi

Nayyar (1989): 'International Migration from India: A Macro-Economic Analysis', in Amjad Rashid (ed), *To the Gulf and Back*, ILO-ARTEP, New Delhi

NITI Aayog (2019): *The Success of Our Schools*, School Education

Quality Index. Government of India, New Delhi

——— (2020): Infant Mortality Rate. http://niti.gov.in/content/infant-mortality-rate-imr-1000-live-births

Oommen, M. A. (2008): 'Microfinance and poverty alleviation: the case of Kerala's Kudumbashree', Centre for Socio-Economic & Environmental Studies, Cochin

——— et al. (2009): 'Report of the Committee for Evaluation of Decentralised Planning and Development', Thiruvananthapuram: Government of Kerala

Pat A.K. (2005): 'Kudumbashree: A Poverty Eradication Mission in Kerala', *Economic and Political Weekly*, Vol. 40, Issue No. 48

Patnaik, Prabhat. (2004): 'A Theoretical Note on Kerala-Style Decentralized Planning'. Macroscan: An Alternative Economics Webcentre. 14 April 2004. https://www.macroscan.org/fet/apr04/fet140404Theoretical_Note_1.htm

P.N.M. Bhat (1995): 'Maternal Mortality in India: Estimates from a Regression Model', Studies in Family Planning, Vol. 26, No. 4

Raj K.N. (1960): 'Approach to Planning of Kerala's Economy', In Omcherry N.N. Pillai (ed), *Planning for Prosperity in Kerala*, The Delhi Malayali Association, New Delhi

——— (1994): 'Has There Been a "Kerala Model"?', International Congress on Kerala Studies, Abstracts, Vol. I, AKG Centre for Research and Studies, Thiruvananthapuram

Rajan, S.I., Zachariah, K.C. (2020): 'New Evidences from the Kerala Migration Survey, 2018'. *Economic and Political Weekly*, January 25, 2020, Vol. 55, Issue No. 4

Raman Kutty V. (2000): 'Historical analysis of the development of health care facilities in Kerala State, India', Health Policy and Planning 15 (1): 103–109

Ramachandran V.K. (1997): 'On Kerala's Development Achievements', in Jean Drèze and Amartya Sen (eds.), *Indian Development: Selected Regional Perspectives*. Oxford University Press, 1997

Sadanandan, R. (2001): 'Government Health Services in Kerala:

Who Benefits?' *Economic and Political Weekly*, Vol. 36, Issue No. 32, pp. 3071–3077

Saradamani, K. (1980): *Emergence of a Slave Caste Pulayar of Kerala*. Peoples Publishing House, New Delhi

Shea W. Thomas (1959): 'The Land Tenure Structure of Malabar and its influence upon Capital Formation in Agriculture', PhD thesis, University of Pennsylvania

Spronk, Susan. (2008): 'Review: Pink Tide? Neoliberalism and Its Alternatives in Latin America'. *Canadian Journal of Latin American and Caribbean Studies* 33(65):173 –186. https://doi.org/10.1080/08263663.2008.10816944

Sreekala M. S. (2010): *1957–59 Varthakalkkappuram*. Chintha Publishers, Thiruvananthapuram

Srinivasan Ramani (2021): 'Excess deaths in Kerala', *The Hindu*, 25 June 2021, Chennai

Thomas Isaac T.M. (1985): 'Class struggle and industrial structure: a study of coir weaving industry in Kerala, 1859–1980', PhD thesis submitted to Jawaharlal Nehru University, Centre for Development Studies, Thiruvananthapuram

———, Tharakan Michael (1986): 'Sree Narayana Movement in Travancore, 1880–1939: A Study of Social Basis and Ideological Reproduction', Working Paper 214, Centre for Development Studies, Thiruvananthapuram

——— (1986): 'The National Movement and the Communist Party in Kerala', *Social Scientist*, Vol. 14, No. 8/9

———, Michael Tharakan, P.K. (1986): 'An Enquiry into the Historical Roots of Industrial Backwardness of Kerala — A Study of Travancore Region', Working Paper 215, Centre for Development Studies, Thiruvananthapuram

———, Ram Manohar Reddy & Nata Duvvury (1992): 'Regional terms of trade for the state of Kerala'. Working paper, 247, Centre for Development Studies, Thiruvananthapuram

———, Ram Manohar Reddy, & Nata Duvvury (1992): 'Balance of trade, remittances and net capital flows: an analysis of economic development in Kerala since independence.' Working paper, 250, Centre for Development Studies, Thiruvananthapuram

——— and P. K. Michael Tharakan. (1995): 'Kerala: Towards a New Agenda', *Economic and Political Weekly* Vol. 30 Issue No. 31–32

——— (2006): 'Why Do the States Not Spend?', *Economic and Political Weekly*, Vol. 41, Issue No. 48

——— (2008): *Vimochana Samarathinte Kanappurangal*. Chintha Publishers, Thiruvananthapuram

———, Lekha Chakraborty, Mohan R. (2019): *Challenges to Indian Fiscal Federalism*. LeftWord Books, New Delhi

——— (2020): 'The Explanation Submitted to Privileges and Ethics Committee of Kerala Legislature Regarding Notice by Sri. V.D. Satheesan, MLA on Breach of Privilege', Vol I & Vol II, (mimeo), 31 November 2020, Office of the Speaker, Kerala Legislative Assembly, Thiruvananthapuram

——— (2020): *Budget Speech 2020–21*, Government of Kerala, Thiruvananthapuram

——— (2021): *Budget Speech 2021–22*, Government of Kerala, Thiruvananthapuram

——— (2021): 'What prevents states from spending', The New Indian Express, 31 December 2021, Chennai

——— and Mathai Ajit (2021): *Coir Kerala – The Agenda for Modernisation*. Centre for Management Development, Thiruvananthapuram

———, and Richard W. Franke (2021): *People's Planning — Kerala, Local Democracy and Development*. LeftWord Books, New Delhi

———, and Williams Michelle (2017): *Building Alternatives The Story of India's Oldest Construction Workers' Cooperative*. LeftWord Books, New Delhi

Thresia, C.U. (2013) 'Rising Private Sector and Falling "Good Health at Low Cost": Health Challenges in China, Sri Lanka and Indian State of Kerala.' *International Journal of Health Services*, vol. 43, no.1, pp. 31–48. https://www. jstor.org/stable/45131943

UNDP (2019): Global Multidimensional Poverty Index 2019, Illuminating Inequalities http://hdr.undp.org/en/2019-MPI

Varghese, T.C. (1970): *Agrarian change and Economics Consequences: Land Tenures in Kerala 1850–1960.* Allied Publishers, Bombay

Vimalan, K. (2019): *Karutharjikkunna Pothu Vidyabhyasam* (Public Education Empowered), Vidyarangam, pp. 20–36. Government of Kerala: General Education Department, Thiruvananthapuram

Zachariah, Mathew and Sooryamoorthy, R. (1994): *Science for Social Action? Achievement and Dilemmas of a Development Movement — The Kerala Sastra Sahitya Parishad.* Vistaar Publications, New Delhi

Zachariah, K.C. and Rajan, S.I. (2016): 'Kerala migration study 2014', *Economic and Political Weekly*, Vol. 51, Issue No. 6. pp. 66–71

Zajda, Joseph (2006): *Decentralization and Privatization in Education — The Role of the State.* Springer, The Netherlands